The American Patriots Series

What people are saying . . .

"Through painstaking and detailed research of primary source documents, Leslie Mironuck has gathered, organized, and produced a superb collection of biographies for readers from middle school upward. . . . clearly shows how the founding fathers guided the framework of the government we have today. The reader will get insight to the individual effort of each founding father as details are shared that are typically omitted from today's textbooks. I wish I had this resource when I started teaching. . . ." *(Excerpt from Foreword)*

— Jim Simmons, M.Ed.
History teacher for 38 years, Mid-Del Schools, OK

"Leslie Mironuck takes readers on his journey of meticulous research to reveal little known facts about the early leaders of our country. Did you know: Joseph Hewes was even part of our history? Benjamin Franklin was one of seventeen children and Patrick Henry fathered seventeen? Israel Putnam's military fame after the French and Indian War equaled that of George Washington? Most public school educators have been guilty of teaching only the high profile Founding Fathers like Hamilton and Jefferson because "there isn't enough time." The majority of the Founders have been ignored . . . until now. Mironuck thoughtfully reintroduces some of these forgotten leaders. It is a journey worth taking."

— Lula Mae Hardman, M.Ed.
Missouri Historical Society's "Teacher of Merit"

"While fantasy superheroes save worlds in the movies, American patriots were real people who took extraordinary actions which resulted in a new country. This chronological three book series details brief biographies of American Revolution patriots—based on primary sources. Each volume is indexed. Bios read like stories and are full of patriot life facts with correlations to American Revolution events. The series is recommended for middle school and high school libraries for support of American history curriculum and History Day activities. Others who will find this series worthwhile are historical storytellers, amateur historians, genealogy buffs, and public libraries."

— Marilyn Odle, M.Ed., M.L.S., School Librarian 30+ years

From Mr. Mironuck's research, using sources from that period, he gives the reader fascinating personal histories of many of the patriots, along with stories of their challenges and courage. Instead of just facts and dates, I read exciting stories about real people, stories that make history come alive, stories I will never forget. Irreconcilable Differences is a "must read."

— Judith Learmann, MA, Former chair Language Arts, Waynesville High School, Adjunct English instructor, Drury College

"Would that I had become an avid reader of American history earlier in life. Mironuck's *Irreconcilable Differences* has stimulated my appetite for discovering more about our Founding Fathers."

— Virgie Cole-Mahan, Ed.D.

"I love the concept of the book and how it focuses on individual Founders and their backgrounds. I especially like the fact that they are not all well known, but still have fascinating stories. Israel Putnam's story was particularly interesting (that guy was really lucky!). The writer has a nice voice and makes the reading enjoyable without "dumbing it down" or becoming too academic. I think the book could be used in an Advanced Placement course."

— Timothy Thieke, High School AP History Teacher

"As I've traveled the nations of the world, I've noticed that the political history within each country is slanted in favor of the country in which it was written. It has been said that written history always favors the victorious nation. While this is true to a degree, I was extremely impressed with the non-biased research in the book, *Irreconcilable Differences* by Leslie Mironuck.

When I received the preliminary manuscript, my intention was to scan through the pages and get a general idea of the content. However, as I began to read, I could not put the manuscript down. It was so insightful and well-written that I sat at length marveling at the magnitude of this work. It revealed details not found in most current historical writings.

The quality of *Irreconcilable Differences*, along with the character and integrity of the author, puts this book in the category of books that should be in every home and library. I want to give my congratulations to the author for this exceptionally excellent work and I look forward to reading his future works in this American Patriot Series, *Liberty or Death* and *Dawn of a Nation*."

— Dr. Larry Ollison, International Speaker, Osage Beach, Missouri

The American Patriots Series

IRRECONCILABLE DIFFERENCES

Profiles of the Founding Fathers
1750 – 1776

Leslie G. Mironuck

Waynesville, MO

Lafayette Publishers
25575 Ridgeview Lane
Waynesville, MO 65583
www.lafayettepublishers.com

ISBN
978-0-9976625-0-4 soft cover
978-0-9976625-1-1 hard cover
978-0-9976625-2-8 e-book

Design: Julie Murkette
www.juliemurkette.com

Publisher's Cataloging-In-Publication Data
(Prepared by The Donohue Group, Inc.)

Names: Mironuck, Leslie G.

Title: Irreconcilable differences : profiles of the Founding Fathers : 1750-1776 / Leslie G. Mironuck.

Other Titles: Profiles of the Founding Fathers : 1750-1776

Description: Waynesville, MO : Lafayette Publishers, [2017] | Series: The American patriots series | Includes bibliographical references and index.

Identifiers: ISBN 978-0-9976625-0-4 (softcover) | ISBN 978-0-9976625-1-1 (hardcover) | ISBN 978-0-9976625-2-8 (ebook)

Subjects: LCSH: Statesmen—United States—History—18th century. | United States—Constitution—Signers. | United States—Politics and government—18th century.

Classification: LCC E302.5 .M57 2017 (print) | LCC E302.5 (ebook) | DDC 973.3/092/2—dc23

Printed in the United States of America

To My Wife:
Oksana Mironuck

And My Children:
Christopher Chad Mironuck
Nicole Danielle Thurman
Tyler James Mironuck

ACKNOWLEDGEMENTS

I would like to thank Dr. Larry Ollison who took the time to read one of my early manuscripts. His endorsement of my book's content was very reassuring, and his encouragement was greatly appreciated. Dr. Larry Ollison is founder and Senior Pastor of Walk on the Water Faith Church and founder of Larry Ollison Ministries. He has been laboring in God's field for over forty years, through radio, television, internet and daily email devotions. Not only has he authored seven books, but he is also a popular speaker on a national and international level.

I am extremely grateful to Judith Learmann, BS, MA, who proofread my manuscript and provided preliminary editorial review. Judith chaired the language arts department at Waynesville High School and was also an adjunct English instructor at Drury College.

I also appreciate the fine work of Reg Parsons and Eva Yatt, the artists who sketched the entire collection of portraits.

And for the finishing touches—the interior layout and the cover artwork—a special thanks to Julie Murkette. I greatly appreciate her subtle creativity and attention to detail.

Thanks to Sharon Castlen, my book marketer and publishing consultant for her valuable direction. She helped me bring out the book I had envisioned and is now moving me forward on the marketing journey.

.

TABLE OF CONTENTS

FOREWORD

by Jim Simmons, M.Ed., retired

Congratulations! Having this book in your hands is a wise choice on your part (or perhaps divine intervention.) Either way, *Irreconcilable Differences* is nothing short of a gift to anyone with even the slightest interest in the patriots who put their fortunes and their lives at risk to provide the blessings of liberty to themselves and their posterity. It is a gift from someone who is more than an author. Leslie Mironuck's passion for American History has become a vocation. Through painstaking and detailed research of primary source documents, he has gathered, organized, and produced a superb collection of biographies for readers from middle school upward. I wish I had this resource when I started teaching. Having retired after 38 years from a career of teaching, I crossed paths with Leslie Mironuck and immediately connected through a love of history. I was honored, pleased, and excited to be offered an opportunity to read the manuscript for this book before it went to print. I am doubly honored and happy to write this foreword.

The author presents the story of American Independence by weaving together the progress and growth of the revolutionary spirit through its people, events, and documents. Details flow seamlessly within the presentation of the contributions and achievements of each of the founding fathers. Their relationships to one another are laid out as pieces of a puzzle, each connecting to several others. Like this book, the revolution itself was well organized. *Irreconcilable Differences* clearly explains colonial efforts to achieve independence and Britain's attempts to prevent it. Mr. Mironuck's talent for writing about the founders of freedom is on par with the best. His work is well-supplied with footnotes and references. Within the text are interesting and appropriately placed quotations and anecdotes.

Irreconcilable Differences clearly shows how the founding fathers guided the framework of the government we have today. The reader will get insight into the individual efforts of each founding father, as details are shared that are typically omitted from today's textbooks. Most students are not even exposed to the scope of the political windings from which our government was created. The richness of each patriot's life is revealed and tied to the common cause. Even before there was such a thing as political parties, colonials were setting precedent for today's leaders.

Biographical information includes ancestors, education, political and military involvement, and post-war activity. Each is concise, yet informative. Examples are given to demonstrate how the founding fathers were honorable, dignified, passionate, and dedicated to the cause of independence. More than once, Mr. Mironuck relates how the wives of our founders made it possible for those men to leave home for extended periods of time to participate in the revolutionary cause. Though this book is not about those women, he is quick to point out their invaluable contribution.

Having read excellent history books by Doris Kearns Goodwin, Jon Meacham, Ken Burns, Ron Chernow, and many others, I would have to say that Leslie Mironuck is an equal. For me, *Irreconcilable Differences* will get multiple readings. It will prove to be a very good reference and resource for history teachers, students and buffs. I found the book to be educational and inspirational. My patriotism is deepened. I personally appreciate that Mr. Mironuck is not worried about the political correctness that prevents many authors from including the deep faith that guided the lives of our founding fathers. As a teacher of American history, I was myself less worried about political correctness and more concerned with the factual information available that showed these people to be human. I am looking forward to reading Volumes II and III of the American Patriot Series. I also would highly recommend that this series of books become a part of any personal collection and school resource room.

— Jim Simmons, M.Ed.

PREFACE

What makes the United States of America such a great nation? The answer to this question is largely found in our rich history. The United States is the longest-running constitutional republic in the history of the world. We have had virtually the same Constitution for well over two hundred years now. Compare that to the eight France has had or the fifty-four Italy has had during the same time frame. Years alone, however, do not provide the main ingredient in our rich history. The main ingredient is traced to our nation's birth, to the great men who won our freedom, framed our founding documents, and set this nation in motion. These men are known as our Founding Fathers.

The Founding Fathers are often alluded to these days, especially when discussing constitutional matters. We often hear that our Founding Fathers would have wanted this or would have intended that. This is an important consideration if we, as a nation, wish to perpetuate our national inheritance. The problem with this consideration is that an alarming number of Americans do not know who the Founding Fathers were, let alone what they stood for. We should not be surprised by this ignorance because the Founding Fathers, as a group, have been absent from the curriculum of our public schools for many decades.

The purpose of this book is to profile America's Founding Fathers so readers may learn who they are, what they stood for, and what their characteristics and beliefs were. Through knowing the Founding Fathers, readers will have a good idea of what they would have wanted and intended for our country. A further benefit of knowing the attributes of our nation's early patriots is that readers can then add those attributes to their own and in so doing, be justified in labeling themselves patriots.

My definition of a Founding Father is one who provided distinguished leadership, exerted significant influence, or substantially impacted the establishment of America during its founding era. My definition will be further limited to the following: the fifty-six signers of the Declaration of Independence, the fourteen presidents of Congress who served prior to our federal Constitution, thirty-three prominent generals who served during the Revolutionary War, the thirty-nine signers of the federal Constitution, the first chief justice of the Supreme Court and his three associate Supreme Court justices, and twenty of the most influential statesmen who helped frame the Bill of Rights. Other patriots like Patrick Henry, James Otis, and Thomas Paine, who are not part of any of the above groups, but still qualify under my broader definition, also will be included. Based on these criteria, I have identified 151 Founding Fathers (150, plus George Washington), whom I will profile in the ensuing pages of this three-volume series. (Please note that the total number of Founders will be less than the sum of the above groups, due to some overlap.)

The readers will benefit from my extensive research. The facts used in writing the following pages were almost completely derived from primary sourced material—the historical books listed in the bibliography. I believe this historical research material is much more reliable than more recently written material because it was written at a time when the facts could have been challenged by eyewitnesses, or in some cases the subjects themselves, if not completely accurate. Also, contemporary research material, for the most part, is nothing more than hearsay. Let me explain what I mean. A historian records an event that took place in his time, which years later is recorded by another historian, which is subsequently recorded by yet another historian, each using the previous source rather than the original source. The result is a modern version of history that is often dramatically distorted from the actual events. It is precisely for this reason that hearsay is not admissible evidence in a court of law. And therefore, hearsay should not be used to rewrite history either.

Two good examples of hearsay—or, generally accepted anecdotes— are the George Washington/cherry tree legend and the allegation that Thomas Jefferson fathered a child with Sally Hemings, one of his slaves. Both of these examples of hearsay have origins that date back more than two hundred years—and nowadays both are generally accepted as factual. The Washington/cherry tree legend first appeared in an elementary school textbook that was used for teaching students lessons about morality. The Jefferson/Hemings allegation first hit the tabloids during Jefferson's presidency, and was written by a political enemy. The former anecdote enhances the reputation of the subject, while the latter piece tarnishes the character of the subject. However, neither of these generally accepted anecdotes qualifies for inclusion in my three-volume series because they weren't mentioned in any of the primary sourced material that I used for my research. These two examples of hearsay are only two among many. The American Patriot Series is fact-based and, therefore, hearsay—rumors, legends, gossip, folklore, and anecdotes—will be ignored.

In an attempt to maintain credibility, I have left most of the quotes used in the original text, including grammar, punctuation, spelling, and the vocabulary consistent with the eighteenth-century lexicon that occasionally may appear foreign to modern readers.

The study of the lives of this great company of men is a study of the history of their time, a time that has become known as the founding era (1750–1799). For obvious reasons, the featured biography in this trilogy will be that of the quintessential George Washington, the father of our country. His public life played a part in almost every major event of the founding era. He served in the 1750s as a general during the French and Indian War, he attended the First Continental Congress, and he was the commander in chief of the Continental Army. He presided over the Constitutional Convention, he became the first president of the United States, and under his leadership, Congress created the Bill of Rights. His death late in 1799 brings a fitting close to the founding era. The profiles of the other Founding Fathers will be inserted into Washington's biography at the time when their lives made a great impact. For example, the biography of Thomas Jefferson will be inserted at the drafting of the Declaration of Independence, and the biography of Thomas Paine will be inserted with the publishing of *Common Sense*.

This volume in *The American Patriots Series* will span the period of 1750 through 1776. It will include the life stories of fifty of the Founding Fathers and describe how they came to grips with their *Irreconcilable Differences* with Great Britain.

TIME LINE: THE FOUNDING ERA
1750-1776

January 30, 1750

Reverend Jonathan Mayhew published his sermon—*Discourse Concerning Unlimited Submission and Non-Resistance to the Higher Powers*—which quietly ushered in the founding era.

July 4, 1754

Colonel George Washington surrendered to the French after a skirmish at Fort Necessity.

July 4, 1754

Benjamin Franklin's *The Albany Plan of Union,* for the defense of the British American colonies, was approved by a special colonial Congress. The plan was similar to the current US Constitution.

July 9, 1755

This date marked the beginning of the French and Indian War. General Edward Braddock set out to conquer the French at Fort Duquesne.

July 13, 1755

The British forces were defeated at Farmington, Pennsylvania, a few miles from Fort Duquesne. General Braddock was killed during the battle. The death of this British general had no impact on the outcome of the French and Indian War.

February 10, 1763

The Treaty of Versailles was signed, bringing an end to hostilities in the French and Indian War. Great Britain became almost the sole mistress of the North American continent.

December 12, 1763

Patrick Henry won the famous legal case known as the Parson's Cause.

May 30, 1765

Patrick Henry delivered his defiant Stamp Act speech in the House of Burgesses. He stated, "If this be treason, make the most of it."

August 14, 1765

Samuel Adams gathered the Sons of Liberty—a group that eventually became the organizational hub of the Northern resistance—under the Liberty Tree in Boston to protest the Stamp Act. This was their first official action.

October 7-25, 1765

Elected representatives from most of the colonies met in New York to discuss the Stamp Act. That gathering became known as the Stamp Act Congress.

June 29, 1767

Parliament enacted the Townshend Act, after which the colonies responded by passing non-importation and non-exportation agreements.

August 1768

Reverend John Witherspoon—father of the Founding Fathers—accepted the presidency of Princeton University. Princeton was eventually called the Seminary of Sedition by many in the British Parliament.

September 5, 1769

A gang of British soldiers attempted to assassinate James Otis.

March 5, 1770

After a scuffle with some Boston youths, a few British soldiers fired shots into the crowd, killing five. The incident became known as the Boston Massacre.

November 2, 1772

Samuel Adams established the first Committee of Correspondence. Almost simultaneously, Richard Henry Lee established a Committee of Correspondence in Virginia. All other colonies eventually followed their example and created their own committees. In doing so, a colonial shadow government was established.

December 16, 1773

In protest of the duties levied by Parliament on tea imported to the colonies, the Sons of Liberty disguised themselves as Indians, boarded three British ships in Boston Harbor, and tossed fifteen thousand pounds of tea overboard. The event became known as the Boston Tea Party.

June 1, 1774

Parliament enacted the Port Act, one of the Intolerable Acts, which closed Boston Harbor.

September 5, 1774

Delegates from twelve colonies met in Philadelphia for the First Continental Congress. They decided to formally—and respectfully—petition the king by way of preparing a list of grievances and violated rights. The petition was then sent to England, after which Congress adjourned.

September 9, 1774

Joseph Warren of Boston authored and presented the Suffolk Resolves to the Massachusetts Assembly. The Resolves declared the Intolerable Acts to be unconstitutional and therefore void. The Resolves spoke against violence and riots, and further declared that the people of Boston would submit only to the authority of Congress.

September 17, 1774

Congress endorsed the Suffolk Resolves.

September 20, 1774

Congress adopted the Articles of Association, which took effect on December 1, 1774.

January 18, 1775

King George III decided not to reply to Congress's petition. Instead, he and Parliament decided to quash the American rebellion.

March 23, 1775

In Virginia, Patrick Henry delivered his "Give me liberty or give me death" speech.

April 19, 1775

The British forces (eighteen hundred soldiers) attacked the colonial militia at Lexington—"the shot heard round the world." The British forces then marched on to Concord, where they were routed by 130 minutemen.

May 10, 1775

The Second Continental Congress convened. The first order of business was to discuss Parliament's response—or lack thereof—to Congress's petition of grievances.

May 10, 1775

Ethan Allen and his eighty-three Green Mountain Boys captured the British fort at Ticonderoga, a remote stronghold in northern New York.

June 15, 1775

Congress commissioned George Washington to be the commander in chief of the Continental Army. He was commissioned to defend the American colonies against British aggression.

June 17, 1775

The British attacked the colonial forces at Bunker Hill. The Royal Army suffered 1,054 casualties, while the colonials lost only 139.

November 12, 1775

General Richard Montgomery completed his congressionally ordered expedition into Canada. He captured the British forts at Chambly, St. John's, and Montreal.

December 31, 1775

Under the leadership of Benedict Arnold, the Continentals were defeated while attempting to capture the British fort at Quebec.

January 9, 1776

Thomas Paine's pamphlet *Common Sense* was released. Tens of thousands of copies were distributed all over the colonies, provoking thousands of previously uncommitted citizens to rethink their neutrality in favor of liberty. Continental Army enlistments skyrocketed.

January 21, 1776
Reverend Peter Muhlenberg delivered an army-recruiting sermon from the pulpit of his Woodstock, Virginia church. He recruited three hundred patriots, men who eventually became the 8th Virginia Brigade. Similar recruiting sermons were delivered throughout the colonies.

March 5, 1776
General Washington chased the British out of Boston Harbor, his first victory, without spilling a drop of blood. The previous night, General Henry Knox had mounted sixty cannons on a hill overlooking Boston. Knox had retrieved the heavy artillery from Fort Ticonderoga.

Spring 1776
Parliament employed nine thousand German mercenaries and sent them, along with over twenty thousand British soldiers, to North America with the intent of snuffing out every vestige of colonial resistance.

June 7, 1776
On the floor of Congress, Richard Henry Lee proposed a resolution for colonial independence.

June 11, 1776
After four days of debate, Congress established a committee to put Lee's resolution in written form. Thomas Jefferson, Lee's protégé and fellow Virginian, was made chairman of the committee, because Lee was absent due to his wife's illness.

June 11, 1776
Congress established a committee—consisting of one member from each colony—to consider, debate, and investigate the question of confederation.

June 28, 1776
Nine British ships of war sailed into Charleston Harbor with the intent of occupying Charleston and immediately came under attack from the South Carolina militia, positioned on Sullivan's Island. After an eleven-hour battle, the defeated British fleet retreated out to sea and returned to New York.

July 4, 1776

Congress voted in favor of the Declaration of Independence, copies of which were sent throughout the colonies, Canada, and Europe.

July 12, 1776

The Confederation Committee completed their assignment and presented their draft articles on the floor of Congress. The articles were debated daily for a month, resulting in a political impasse. It was decided that before progress could be made, all the state governments needed to be organized and solidified.

August 2, 1776

A signing ceremony was held on the floor of Congress—each of the delegates present signed the Declaration.

Introduction

The purpose of the following biographies is to familiarize ourselves with the Founding Fathers. However, before we begin to study the primary participants of the founding era, I believe it is imperative that we understand the theater in which they acted and the circumstances that brought them to that point in history.

The discovery of America, as far as the Europeans are concerned, occurred in 1492, when Christopher Columbus stumbled upon the West Indies during his first highly controversial, but providential, exploratory expedition to the extremities of the Atlantic Ocean. The purpose of that voyage is described in his writings:

> Our Lord opened to my understanding (I could sense his hand upon me) so it became clear to me that it [the voyage] was feasible . . . All those who heard about my enterprise rejected it with laughter, scoffing at me . . . Who doubts that this illumination was from the Holy Spirit? I attest that He [the Spirit], with marvelous rays of light consoled me through the holy and sacred Scriptures . . . they inflame me with a sense of great urgency . . . No one should be afraid to take on any enterprise in the name of our Savior if it is right and if the purpose is purely for His holy service . . . And I say that the sign which convinces me that our Lord is hastening the end of the world is the preaching of the Gospel recently in so many lands.[1]

Columbus's well-publicized discovery encouraged other explorers, financed by other European countries—as well as by private entities—to set out and stake their claims in the new continent. Brave and determined settlers who were motivated by their desire for religious liberty subsequently colonized those claims. This is evident by the Mayflower Compact, the governing charter drafted by the Pilgrims, who in 1620 landed in Massachusetts Bay, which became the first permanent settlement in America. It states,

Having undertaken for the glory of God and advancement of the Christian faith . . . [we] combine ourselves together into a civil body politic for . . . furthermore of the ends aforesaid.[2]

About a decade later, the Puritans arrived in America under the leadership of John Winthrop, who declared,

We are a company professing ourselves fellow-members of Christ . . . Knit together by this bond of love . . . we are entered into covenant with Him for this work . . . for we must consider that we shall be as a city upon a hill, the eyes of all people are upon us.[3]

In 1636, Roger Williams, an Anabaptist minister whose Christian views were too radical to be welcome in New England, purchased land from the Indians and established Providence, Rhode Island. The charter of Rhode Island eventually stated,

Pursuing with peace and loyal minds, their sober, serious and religious intentions of Godly edifying themselves and one another in the holy Christian faith . . . a most flourishing civil state may stand and best be maintained . . . with a full liberty in religious concernments.[4]

In 1653, the Quakers settled in Carolina, and their charter stated,

Excited with laudable and pious zeal for the propagation of the Christian faith . . . in the parts of America not yet cultivated or planted, and only inhabited by . . . people who have no knowledge of Almighty God.[5]

The Anglicans, along with the Calvinists and Methodists, settled in Virginia. William Penn, a Quaker, established Philadelphia, the City of Brotherly Love, and promised the Lutherans and Catholics freedom of worship within the colony. As a result, America was being flooded by Christian settlers of various sects, who by the courage of their convictions took responsibility for their future and left England (as well as other European countries) in pursuit of their religious liberties.

Christianity continued to flourish in America through the remainder of the seventeenth century and eventually birthed the Great Awakening in 1740. That movement attracted evangelical titans such as George Whitefield and John and Charles Wesley to America. The revival intensified the dissenting bias that already existed against church hierarchy in Great Britain and initiated the breaking down of the walls of separation between the many different Christian denominations, which helped unite the colonies. The dissenting bias against church hierarchy carried over and sparked a similar bias against British government hierarchy and monarchism. It was from the pulpit that the first argument was made against British tyranny. The argument was made—and justified—by scripture. The pulpit belonged to Reverend Jonathan Mayhew, a Harvard graduate called the prophet of the American Revolution by many historians. His landmark sermon was given in 1750 and quietly ushered in the founding era.

At the beginning of the founding era, America led the world in education and social economics. Colleges such as Harvard, Yale, Princeton, and William & Mary had been established as seminaries, and as such, all graduates were considered theologians. Scholarships and tuition work programs were offered liberally, availing higher education to commoners, which resulted in more college graduates per population than any other country in the world. Nine out of ten adults owned land, and unemployment was almost nonexistent, creating a ballooning middle class and a firm foundation for capitalism.

Through immigration and procreation, the population of the various colonies grew at a rate that far outpaced their transatlantic counterparts. With each passing year, the colonists became more and more economically important to their homelands. From the late seventeenth century until 1754, two of the great world powers, Great Britain and France, struggled for control of the vast lands of America. At that time, the English controlled most of the coastal regions, but very little of the interior. France had settled north of the Saint Lawrence River in the territory that is today part of eastern Canada, as well as in Louisiana and throughout the Mississippi Valley areas that linked its northern and southern colonies. The French strategy was to surround the English colonies and cut them off from settling west of the Appalachians, which if successful, would leave France with the greater part of America.

In 1755, the final conflict for American supremacy erupted and became known to the English colonies as the French and Indian War. The English colonies obviously allied with Great Britain, and the Indians sided with France. Previously, the colonies always had acted independently of each other, each having their separate governments, religion, cultures, and so on. But for the first time, the individual colonies rallied together to oppose one common foe.

The colonial troops made several valuable observations during the French and Indian War. First, their many perceived differences were diminished by their shared patriotism. Second, although the British troops had more military training, the militias from the various colonies outperformed them, presumably because they were defending their families and personal property. In the years to come, while contemplating independence, those observations would help to build the confidence of the American people.

PART I

The Stage Is Set

A HERO IS BORN

George Washington
February 22, 1732 – July 4, 1754

The family name of "Wassyngton"—the ancient spelling of "Washington"—had been prominent in Durham County, England, as early as the twelfth century. In 1529, Lawrence Washington relocated to Northamptonshire, where he became a successful wool merchant. Lawrence acquired an estate-type property and built a large house that he named Sulgrave Manor. The manor remained in the family holdings for at least fifty years. Lawrence Washington's great-grandson and namesake was born at the family seat in 1604. Young Lawrence was given an excellent education, culminating in his theology degree from Brasenose College, Oxford, in 1623. Soon after receiving his degree, he became the rector[a] of a parish in Purleigh, a small village in Essex County, where he later married and started a family. Lawrence's son, John—the great-grandfather of George Washington—was born in 1634.

---

[a] Lawrence's career in the ministry was not unusual for the Washington clan. In fact, working in God's field was a well-established tradition in the Washington family lineage. As proof of that fact, consider that the Washington family coat of arms is displayed on a stained glass window in a fifteenth-century monastery located in Yorkshire, England.

At age twenty-three, John Washington emigrated from Northern England and arrived in Virginia, where he settled down and married Anne Pope. Anne's father, Colonel Nathaniel Pope, was a wealthy plantation owner who gave the happy couple some land in Westmoreland County as a wedding gift. John put the land to good use and became a successful agriculturalist. The young couple soon built a modest four-room house that became known as Wakefield, the place where the next few generations of descendants would be born. John expanded his interests to include politics and military tactics—serving in the House of Burgesses and as a colonel in the Virginia militia.

In September 1659, Anne gave John a son, the first of the Washington clan to be born in America. They named him Lawrence, after his paternal grandfather. Being the firstborn, much attention was given to the lad's education. His parents sent him to England, where he studied law. At the completion of his education, Lawrence returned to Virginia and became a lawyer and, like his father, he also found time to become involved in politics. It is presumed that he primarily focused his attention on his career and politics, as the family's landholdings did not expand under his watch. However, he did find time to pursue romance, which resulted in his marriage to Mildred Warner in 1688. They eventually increased their family by the addition of three children: John, Augustine, and Mildred. During the same year that Mildred was born, Lawrence died. He was only thirty-eight years old.

At Wakefield in 1694, Augustine, the father of George Washington, was born. Augustine—or "Gus," as his friends and neighbors referred to him—was much like his grandfather, John, in that he was tall, possessed great physical strength, and was a shrewd land trader. Gus eventually expanded the family's landholdings to include a 2,500-acre parcel of land on Little Hunting Creek, later known as Mount Vernon. In 1715, Gus married Jane Butler, and they had four children. However, only two survived to reach maturity: Lawrence and Augustine Jr. Four years after Jane's death in 1729, Gus married Mary Ball, who was fourteen years his junior. Gus and Mary had five children; their firstborn was George Washington.

George Washington—the father of our nation—was born on February 22, 1732. Young George's childhood years were split between his many tedious farm chores and his education, which was limited to about five years in a common country school. It appears that he then continued his education under the tutelage of his elder half-brother, Lawrence, who had been educated in England. George became skilled at handwriting and developed proficiencies in mathematics, trigonometry, and geometry. Those skills eventually helped him launch an early, short-lived career in surveying. His other areas of interest included geography, climatology, astronomy, and history. George also enjoyed reading and spent much of his time devouring all the popular books of his day.

When George was ten years old, his father died, cutting short his childhood and forcing him to mature quickly and to concentrate on his education. A few years later, George went to live with Lawrence, who by that time had married and had built his own house on a parcel of the Mount Vernon property. Lawrence's wife, Anne, was the daughter of Lord Thomas Fairfax, a British nobleman. While living with his half-brother, George became acquainted with Fairfax and eventually developed a close friendship with him. Fairfax hired George, who had been apprenticing as a surveyor, to map out his extensive landholdings, which extended more than a hundred miles west.

As George surveyed the land, he became familiar with the frontier by studying its topography, dealing with the Indians, and learning wilderness survival. He also gained the experience necessary to become a government surveyor, an occupation that paid very well. When the governor of Virginia, Robert Dinwiddie, heard how pleased Fairfax was with George's work, he made George a public surveyor.

George's employment with Governor Dinwiddie opened new career doors. At nineteen, the six-foot-three-inch-tall George Washington was appointed one of the adjutant generals of Virginia, with the rank of major. Less than two years later, the government commissioned him for a mission that would require both the prudence of a senior statesman and the vigor of his youth. The governor of Virginia sent Washington to deliver an ultimatum to the French military, which had begun to occupy the Ohio Valley. The royal message to the French was to leave British soil or suffer the consequences.

In November 1753, George set out on his mission with his guide, Christopher Gist, a lifelong friend. The thousand-mile expedition would take them through the vast wilderness of the interior during the dead of winter. After delivering the message, he returned home; the entire journey had taken only two and one-half months. Upon hearing the exciting details of the mission, Dinwiddie was so impressed that he had George's journal published. *The Journal of Major General Washington* was so widely read that the twenty-one-year-old Washington became the most celebrated hero in Virginia.

When the French responded negatively to the ultimatum, the Virginia Assembly raised a regiment of three hundred men for the purpose of defending the colony's frontier. Washington was appointed lieutenant colonel and sent out, in the spring of 1754, to expel the French from Fort Duquesne.[b] After weeks of marching, Washington was only sixty miles from his destination when he received intelligence that the French were en route to attack his regiment. Finding a clearing, a spot known as the Great Meadows, he constructed a small makeshift stockade that he appropriately named Fort Necessity. Prior to its completion, twelve hundred French soldiers surrounded the fort and proceeded to open fire upon the Virginia militia. After a daylong siege, Washington was forced to surrender. On July 4, 1754, favorable terms of capitulation were negotiated, and the brave soldiers were allowed to return to Virginia. Once home, they received public thanks from the Virginia House of Burgesses for the bravery they demonstrated against such overwhelming odds.

During the same day that Colonel George Washington was negotiating his terms of surrender with his French enemy, his future friend and fellow statesman from Pennsylvania, Benjamin Franklin, had his Plan of Union for the defense of the British-American colonies approved by a special colonial congress that had gathered in Albany, New York.

---

[b] The city of Pittsburgh was eventually built on the same site.

Benjamin Franklin

Josiah Franklin, the father of Benjamin Franklin, was a devout Puritan who, with his wife and three children, fled England in 1682 in search of religious freedom. He settled in Boston, where he took up the trades of soap-boiler and candle-maker. After the death of his first wife, he married Miss Abiah Folger, the daughter of Peter Folger, one of the first settlers in New England. Who would have suspected that this rather obscure family would produce one of the world's greatest and most respected intellectuals?

Benjamin Franklin was born in Boston on January 17, 1706. The third youngest of seventeen children (all of whom survived to maturity), Benjamin remembered eating at the same table with as many as thirteen children. Because his parents hoped young Benjamin would become a Gospel minister, they took an early interest in his education and taught him to read at a very young age. Benjamin characterized his precociousness, "My early readiness in learning to read (which must have been very early, as I do not remember when I could not read) . . . ."[1] However, due to poor finances, his schooling was cut short and limited to two years. This turned out to be an advantage for Benjamin, because he was forced to direct his own studies, and no formal boundaries or finish lines were established for his education.

He later began working in his father's business, but he did not like that occupation, so he switched to an apprenticeship in the printing business under an elder brother. He excelled in that profession, but all the while he remained studious, spending all of his idle time with his nose buried in a book. At seventeen, Franklin set out on his own to make his mark in life. He was lured to New York City because of its thriving economy. Not finding any work there, he moved on to Philadelphia, the largest city in the colonies. He arrived alone, without a friend and with only one dollar in his pocket. He was pleased to discover the city full of opportunity, and he quickly found employment as a typesetter.

Within a few years, his character, Puritan work ethic, and talents earned him many friends, the confidence and respect of the public, and a partnership in a printing business. In 1730, Franklin married Deborah Read, described as "a handsome woman of comely figure, yet nevertheless industrious and frugal."[2] Together they had two children, a boy and a girl. Over the years, Benjamin Franklin made many contributions to both Philadelphia and the American colonies.

In 1732, Franklin began to publish his *Poor Richard's Almanack*, which was widely circulated in the colonies and Europe for several decades and eventually translated into many languages. About the same time, he established a colonial newspaper that became highly popular. He also published numerous pamphlets that included essays on all the pressing issues of the day. A few of these pamphlets were authored by the influential British evangelist George Whitefield. Each publication seemed to add to Franklin's fame. Franklin also became an occasional financial supporter of Whitefield, writing in his autobiography,

> I happened soon after to attend one of [Whitefield's] sermons, in the course of which I perceived he intended to finish with a collection, and I silently resolved he should get nothing from me. I had in my pocket a handful of copper money, three or four silver dollars, and five pistols in gold. As he proceeded I began to soften, and concluded to give him the coppers. Another stroke of his oratory made me ashamed of that, and determined me to give the silver, and he finished so admirably, that I emptied my pocket wholly into the collector's dish, gold and all.[3]

In 1734, the governor appointed Franklin to be the official government printer. Two years later, he was appointed the clerk of the General Assembly, followed a year later by a promotion to postmaster of Philadelphia. These many posts translated into financial gain, employees, and more leisure time, which Franklin used for philosophical pursuits and civic advancements. He organized the United States' first fire department and devised the means to pave and light city streets. He established the first public library in Philadelphia and presented proposals for the American Philosophical Society, Pennsylvania Hospital, and Pennsylvania University. In 1742, he invented a unique stove that became known as the Franklin stove. He donated the design of the stove to the general public.

In 1744, after serving as justice of the peace and city alderman, Franklin was elected a member of the Provincial General Assembly, a position he held for ten consecutive years. During those years, he also found time to conduct experiments with electricity, discovering some of its many properties, which led to his inventing the lightning rod. His work with electricity gained him universal fame and an honorary doctorate from one of the oldest colleges in Scotland.

As the French began to encroach upon the British American colonies in the early part of the 1750s, it became apparent that a union of the colonies was absolutely necessary for their preservation. A congress was called in Albany, consisting of one delegate each from Massachusetts, New York, New Hampshire, Rhode Island, Connecticut, Maryland, and Pennsylvania. On June 14, 1754, Franklin arrived in Albany as Pennsylvania's delegate. After completing a treaty with the Indians of the Six Nations, the question of uniting the colonies into a common government was then raised and addressed. Franklin subsequently submitted a plan titled the Albany Plan of Union. The plan was surprisingly similar to America's current Constitution.

The Albany Plan proposed that the new government would have joint representatives of the king and of the colonial assemblies and would include a president who possessed the power to declare war and peace, negotiate treaties, and regulate trade. The president also would be vested with the authority to establish new colonies and create new laws, as well as the power to impose taxes. All, however, would be subject to the king's approval. Franklin's plan was thoroughly debated and finally agreed upon. On July 4, 1754, the plan was signed by all the delegates. The signing date was exactly twenty-two years—to the day—before the Declaration of Independence would be signed. Copies of the plan were then sent to each of the colonies and to the king for his approval. Both parties subsequently rejected the plan, but for opposite reasons: the king and his Parliament because it contained too many democratic ideas, and the colonies because the king retained too much power. Those events foreshadowed and perhaps provided a glimpse at the conflicts that lay ahead between America and Great Britain.

In 1757, the General Assembly of Pennsylvania sent Franklin to London as its representative in a dispute with the governor. His diplomacy proved to be so effective in obtaining a verdict in favor of the colony that he was requested to remain in England as a resident agent for Pennsylvania. His commission lasted for five years, and upon his return to Philadelphia, he was publicly thanked and awarded $20,000, compensation for a job well done.

During the turbulent Stamp Act era, Franklin was once again asked to appear before the British Parliament on behalf of American interests. His loud and bold protests were respectfully received and accomplished much for the colonial cause. He remained in England as a constant advocate for America until 1775, when he perceived the inevitability of war and consequently returned home. Once back in Philadelphia, he was immediately elected to the Continental Congress. He was later appointed to the committee whose task it was to draft the Declaration of Independence, a document he proudly signed on August 2, 1776.

After independence was proclaimed, Congress recommended that each state establish a new government. Pennsylvania called for a constitutional convention and chose Franklin as its president. His wisdom and leadership facilitated a rapid and successful conclusion to the convention. Then at age seventy, having had a full political career, one might think that he would consider retirement. Instead, Franklin accepted Congress's call to aid in foreign affairs and immediately sailed for France, intent on negotiating a treaty of alliance. In February 1778, after the news of America's stunning victory at Saratoga, Franklin's mission reached fruition. Five years later, at the conclusion of the Revolutionary War, Franklin had the pleasure of signing the Treaty of Peace with Great Britain.[c]

With peace secured, Franklin requested a leave from Congress so that he might return to his family in America. Although his request was granted,

---

[c] John Adams and John Jay also signed the Treaty of Peace.

he was detained until Thomas Jefferson, his successor, arrived in 1785. America received his return with great adulation, and in appreciation he was appointed president of Pennsylvania, an office he held for three years.

During the summer of 1787, Franklin attended the Constitutional Convention, where being over eighty years of age, he filled the role of senior statesman. It was in that capacity, and at a period when high emotions and different opinions threatened the demise of the convention, that he addressed the delegates:

Mr. President [George Washington]

The small progress we have made after four or five weeks of close attendance & continual reasonings with each other—our different sentiments on almost every question, several of the last producing as many noes as ayes, is methinks a melancholy proof of the imperfection of the Human Understandings. We indeed seem to feel our own want of political wisdom, since we have been running about in search of it. We have gone back to ancient history for models of Government, and examined the different forms of those Republics which have been formed with the seeds of their own dissolution now no longer exist. And we have viewed modern States all around Europe, but find none of their Constitutions suitable to our circumstances.

In this situation of the Assembly, groping as it were in the dark to find political truth, and scarce able to distinguish it when presented to us, how has it happened, Sir, that we have not hitherto once thought of humbly applying to the Father of lights to illuminate our understandings? In the beginning of the Contest with Great Britain, when we were sensible of danger we had daily prayer in this room for the divine protection.—Our prayers, Sir, were heard, & they were graciously answered. All of us who were engaged in the struggle must have observed frequent instances of a superintending providence in our favor. To that kind providence we owe this happy opportunity of consulting in peace on the means of establishing our future national felicity. And have we now forgotten that powerful friend? Or do we imagine that we no longer need His assistance? I have lived, Sir, a long time, and the longer I live, the more convincing proofs I see of this truth—that God Governs in the affairs of men. And if a sparrow cannot fall to the ground without his notice, is it probable that an empire can rise without his aid? We have been assured, Sir, in the sacred writings, that 'except the Lord build the House they labour in vain that build it.' I firmly believe this; and I also believe that without his concurring aid we shall succeed in this political building no better, than the Builders of Babel: We shall be divided by our little partial local interests; our projects will be confounded, and we ourselves shall become a reproach and bye word down to future ages. And what is worse, mankind may hereafter from this unfortunate instance, despair of establishing Governments by Human wisdom and leave it to chance, war and conquest.

I therefore beg leave to move—that henceforth prayers imploring the assistance of Heaven, and its blessings on our deliberations, be held in this Assembly every morning before we proceed to business, and that one or more of the Clergy of this City be requested to officiate in that Service.[4]

The attendees all recognized Franklin's wisdom. At the conclusion of the convention, he placed his signature upon the Constitution, which was the last public duty he performed. Dr. Benjamin Franklin, who died on April 17, 1790, at eighty-four, was mourned throughout America and Europe with profound grief. Over twenty thousand grateful countrymen followed his remains in a vast funeral procession to his burial site. One month before his death, Franklin wrote the following to Ezra Stiles, a Congregational minister and the president of Yale College:

Here is my creed. I believe in one God, Creator of the Universe. That he governs it by his Providence. That he ought to be worshipped. That the most acceptable service we render to Him is doing good to His other children. That the soul of man is immortal, and will be treated with justice in another life respecting its conduct in this. These I take to be the fundamental principles of all sound religion, and I regard them as you do in whatever sect I meet with them.

As to Jesus of Nazareth, my opinion of whom you particularly desire, I think the system of morals and his religion, as he left them to us, the best the world ever saw or is likely to see.[5]

THE FRENCH AND INDIAN WAR

George Washington

July 1755

In 1755, the British retaliated for the French attack on George Washington at Fort Necessity by sending an army to America, marking the beginning of the French and Indian War.[d] The army, under the leadership of General Edward Braddock, consisted of twenty-three hundred battle-ready soldiers, who were well trained in European war tactics. In addition, the British forces were bolstered by the various colonial militias, which were led by such men as George Washington, Thomas Gage, Horatio Gates, Charles Lee, and Israel Putnam.[e] On July 9, 1755, Braddock set out with thirteen hundred soldiers to conquer Fort Duquesne, the infamous French stronghold. Braddock commissioned Colonel Washington, and his band of a hundred Virginia buckskins, to accompany him.

Knowing that the European form of battle was inappropriate for the American frontier, Washington warned Braddock and made him aware of the unconventional Indian methods of war. Braddock paid no attention to the inferior American colonel and proceeded normally, but things soon went terribly awry. When Braddock's troops were only a few miles from their destination and marching through a thickly wooded ravine, they were ambushed. The French and Indians fired upon them from both sides. The surprised European veterans of war had no idea what to do. They had fought only in open fields, where they lined up and shot at the enemy, who was in plain view. In all the mayhem, they did exactly what they

---

[d] The "French and Indian War" is the name that the British colonists gave to the conflict. However, the French colonists referred to the conflict as the "War of the Conquest."

[e] All these generals eventually became commanders in the War of Independence.

had been trained to do: they stood shoulder to shoulder and fired at the enemy. However, their new frontier enemy seemed to be invisible. After two hours of battle, the French and Indians had lost only 30 men, while the British and American troops had suffered 714 casualties, including General Braddock. Colonel Washington was the only officer, out of eighty-six, still on horseback.

After retreating back to Fort Cumberland, Washington wrote to his mother:

> July 18, 1755
> Honored Madam:
> As I doubt not but you have heard of our defeat, and perhaps had it represented in a worse light, if possible, than it deserves. I have taken this earliest opportunity to give you some account of the engagement as it happened, within ten miles of the French fort, on Wednesday the 9th . . . .
> The General was wounded, of which he died three days after. Sir Peter Halkett was killed in the field, where he died with many other brave officers. I luckily escaped without a wound, though I had four bullets through my coat, and two horses shot under me . . . I am, honored Madam, your most dutiful son.
> G. Washington

He wrote his brother, John A. Washington, on the same day:

> As I have heard, since my arrival at this place [Fort Cumberland], a circumstantial account of my death and dying speech. I take this early opportunity of contradicting the first, and of assuring you, that I have not as yet composed the latter. But, by the all-powerful dispensations of Providence, I have been protected beyond all human probability or expectation; for I had four bullets through my coat, and two horses shot under me, yet escaped unhurt, although death was leveling my companions on every side of me![6]

Fifteen years later in 1770, George Washington, accompanied by a contingent of French and Indian War veterans, returned to that same battlefield, where he met an old Indian chief who, upon hearing of his return, traveled many miles to meet him. They sat down together over a council fire, and the chief then told Washington,

> I am a chief and ruler over my tribes. My influence extends to the waters of the great lakes and to the far blue mountains. I have traveled a long and weary path that I might see the young warrior of the great battle. It was on the day when the white man's blood mixed with the streams of our forest that I first beheld this chief [Washington]. I called to my young men and said, mark yon tall and daring warrior? He is not of the red-coat tribe—he hath an Indian's wisdom, and his warriors fight as we do—himself is alone exposed. Quick, let your aim be certain, and he dies. Our rifles were leveled, rifles which, but for you, knew not how to miss—'twas all in vain, a power mightier far than we, shielded you. Seeing you were under the special guardianship of the Great Spirit, we immediately ceased to fire at you. I am old and soon shall be gathered to the great council fire of my fathers in the land of shades, but ere I go, there is something bids me speak in the voice of prophecy. Listen! The Great Spirit protects that man [pointing at Washington], and guides his destinies—he will become the chief of nations, and a people yet unborn will hail him founder of a mighty empire. I am come to pay homage to the man who is the particular favorite of Heaven, and who can never die in battle.[7]

The old Indian's prophecy spoke truth. George Washington was never wounded in any battle. Some years later during an excavation of the battle site, one of George Washington's brass vest buttons (inscribed with his initials) was found—a musket ball imprint on its side.

The defeat and death of General Braddock had little effect on the outcome of the French and Indian War. After eight years of hostilities, Great Britain gained possession of all the French-held regions in America, which included the settlements in Canada and the French settlements in New Orleans and up the Mississippi Valley. At the same time, Great Britain acquired East and West Florida from Spain through a trade—Britain gave up Cuba. Those events made Great Britain the sole mistress of the populated areas in North America.

Israel Putnam

Larger than life and full of intrigue would be a close description of the much-celebrated military career of General Putnam, the hero of two American wars. His notoriety following the French and Indian War was second only to that of George Washington. After the war, like Washington, he laid down his instruments of war and retired to a quiet and peaceful existence on his farm, but when the British guns shattered America's security at Concord, they beckoned him to their defense. Even though he was fifty-seven years of age, Putnam obediently answered his country's call. After displaying his vintage heroics at Bunker Hill, it was obvious that he was destined to maintain his gallant reputation throughout the War of Independence. A crippling stroke, however, prohibited a repeat performance of his earlier glory years.

The Putnams were among the first colonists to arrive in America. In the latter part of the seventeenth century, John Putnam and his two brothers emigrated from the south of England and settled in Salem, Connecticut. John's son, Captain Joseph Putnam, had established the family dynasty by the time Israel was born. Israel Putnam was born on January 7, 1718. He grew up on his father's farm near Salem, and as most youngsters reared from that hardy stock, he received only a limited education (a shame, because the boy possessed a vigorous and curious mind). His years of physical labor equipped him with a solid frame, which was clad with a thick layer of muscle. He excelled in sports of all types and almost always finished first. Courage and tenacity were the hallmarks of his character. He once followed a wolf, responsible for killing seventy of his sheep, back to its den and then with a torch in one hand and a gun in the other, entered the blackened cave and slew the predator. Though he was a rugged man, he did have a gentle side, and it was that combination that in 1738 won him the hand of Miss Hannah Pope—his hometown sweetheart. They established their home on a farm near Pomfret, Connecticut, where they raised seven children, three boys and four girls.

For almost twenty years, he enjoyed the fruits of his chosen vocation, but in 1755, when the long-standing feud with the French erupted into an intercontinental war, he volunteered to help defend his country. Putnam, at thirty-seven, was in the prime of his life. Due to his reputation, he immediately received the command of a small company of the Connecticut militia that, along with a division of General Braddock's army, was dispatched to the northern frontier. Over the next two years, he saw action at Lake George and Lake Champlain, and during those campaigns, he was promoted to captain and then to major.

During the summer of 1757, he and a small company of rangers were dispatched on an ill-fated expedition to Ticonderoga to scout the enemy. While trudging through the forest, they came across a band of natives. The ensuing battle resulted in Putnam being captured and his comrades taking flight. The Indians, not bound by any civilized rules of war, decided to burn their prisoner alive. They stripped him, tied him to a tree, piled brush and logs around his feet, and set the wood afire while Putnam watched with the firmness of one unafraid to face death. Providentially, the skies began to pour down rain and extinguished the fire. When the heavenly downpour finally ceased, the frustrated Indians revived the flame only to have the showers return. The cycle continued again and again, until at length, the clouds moved on. The undaunted braves gleefully continued with their plans. They reignited the brush and began to dance ceremoniously around their fearless victim. Then, when Putnam's demise seemed inevitable, a French patrol came upon the scene and put an end to the attempted atrocity. Putnam was seized as a prisoner of war and escorted to Montreal, where he was eventually released through a prisoner exchange.

News of his near-death encounter and bravery spread rapidly through-out the colonies, and the name of Putnam soon became a household word. In 1759, he was promoted to lieutenant colonel in the British Army and reassigned to the northern forces where he was immediately dispatched on an important expedition. The campaign was successful and resulted in the capture of the forts at Ticonderoga and Crown Point. He continued to perform gallantly throughout the northern frontier until the close of the war. At that time, Putnam sought not to capitalize on his fame by advancing his military career; instead, he slipped into obscurity by returning to the repose of his family and farm.

The tranquility and afterglow of the war did not last long as Britain, then the dominant world power, began flexing its newly found muscle. Being a patriot, Colonel Putnam turned his back on the Crown and sided with the common folk in their rejection of the Stamp Act. As the turbulent years leading up to Lexington unraveled, Putnam became an increasingly loud voice for American liberty.

In 1767, Putnam, a forty-nine-year-old widower, married Deborah Gardiner, the widow of Lord Gardiner. At the time of that high-society marriage, Putnam was already a man of substantial net worth, a veteran in the provincial legislature, and, of course, still well respected as a military hero. With his fame and his bride's social connections, his home became a constant stopping place for "relatives, friends, traveling ministers, distinguished strangers, and gushing patriots"[8] who were passing through the area. The financial burden of his hospitality became immense. Putnam, always a shrewd businessman, decided to turn a profit on the situation and opened a country inn[f] on his estate. He and Mrs. Putnam made their permanent residence there.

The day after the British battled the minutemen at Lexington, Putnam, unaware of the event, was busy working in his fields when from a distance he noticed a man on a horse galloping toward him. As the rider approached, Putnam heard the sound of a rapidly beaten drum and recognized the call to battle. The messenger, once within earshot, blurted, "The streets of Lexington and Concord have been soaked in blood, and the country is in blaze."[9] Without a moment's hesitation, the old warrior mounted his steed and left for Cambridge. He arrived the next day, having traversed a hundred miles in just twenty-four hours, and immediately called for a council of

---

[f] The inn was like a modern-day bed and breakfast.

war. After a stern and motivating speech, appealing to the patriotism of those in attendance, he explained the need to stand firm against their royal antagonist. He then hurried off to the Assembly of Connecticut. The members were briefed, and plans for Connecticut's defense were adopted. Putnam was appointed brigadier general of the provincial militia. He then returned to his home, put on his old uniform, dug out his firearms and rusty sword, said farewell to his family, and set out to raise a regiment. The men of Connecticut poured in to serve under their great leader. His moral authority was second to none, and his men knew that the enemy feared him because he feared nothing. General Putnam and his company arrived in Cambridge to join other forces from every quarter of the land. With no one having more experience than Israel Putnam, he gradually assumed command of the whole. To build their confidence, Putnam drilled his troops constantly and constructed fortifications on the hills surrounding Boston. The preparations paid dividends as the colonials performed admirably against the redcoats during the Battle of Bunker Hill.

Meanwhile, Congress had appointed George Washington as commander in chief of the Continental Army and named Putnam as one of his four major generals. From that time forth, Major General Putnam served his commander faithfully and diligently. In the fall of 1777, when Putnam wrote Washington to announce the surrender of General Burgoyne, he added this postscript: "I have the unhappiness to inform you that Mrs. Putnam, after a long and tedious illness, departed this life last Tuesday night." Washington replied,

> To Major General Putnam:
> Your favor of the 26th I received yesterday morning and was much obliged for the interesting contents. The defeat of General Burgoyne is a most important event . . . I am extremely sorry for the death of Mrs. Putnam and sympathise with you upon the occasion. Remember that all must die, and that she lived to an honourable age. I hope you bear the misfortune with that fortitude and complacency of mind that becomes a man and a Christian.
> I am, dear sir, with great pleasure, yours,
> George Washington[10]

Late in 1779, after the army had entered their winter quarters at Morristown, Putnam took leave to visit his family. The much-needed extended furlough was ended with the coming of spring. As the sixty-one-year-old general journeyed toward his military headquarters, at a spot just before Hartford, he suffered a stroke that left him with permanent paralysis, putting an abrupt end to his extraordinary military career. Although an invalid, he felt blessed to live an additional ten years because he was able to witness not only the successful end to the war, but also the establishment of the federal Constitution and his old friend, George Washington, elected to the presidency. The veteran hero died on May 17, 1790, confident of his afterlife reward. Sometime prior to his death, he had stood up in the Congregational Church, in Brooklyn, Connecticut—where he was a regular member—and publically confessed his sins and asked for forgiveness. The contrite Putnam admitted that he had used foul language at the Battle of Bunker Hill. He explained that he had been frustrated with his timid militia and that "it was almost enough to make an angel swear, to see the cowards refuse to secure a victory so nearly won." One of his early biographers described his character as follows:

> An iron man, he nevertheless had as kind a heart as ever beat in a human bosom. His reckless and adventurous life never hardened his feelings or produced that rigidity of character which seems at first unavoidable. He was generous to a fault, frank and confiding, and of unswerving integrity. With all his impulsiveness his nature was sincere and firm. Beloved by all who knew him, faithful to every trust committed to his charge, a devoted patriot, and a brave and noble man, he helped to fill up the measure of his country's glory, and received the blessings of a grateful people.[11]

THE PARSON'S CAUSE

George Washington

1755-1763

After Colonel Washington's heroics and immortality were demonstrated during the French and Indian ambush near Fort Duquesne, his anecdotal fame spread throughout America and Europe, causing his military career to flourish. He was promoted to commander of all Virginia troops, and so great was the public confidence in his judgment that he was extended the privilege of naming his own field officers.

During the latter part of 1758, Washington set out with his troops to erase a blemish that he felt had tarnished his career. He returned to Fort Duquesne to once and for all expel the French from their last frontier stronghold. To his great surprise, the fort was unoccupied, as the French had just previously retreated down the Ohio River. He seized the fort, which for the remainder of the war proved to be a valuable asset to the British.

After the campaign of 1758 ended and the capture of Fort Duquesne had been accomplished, Washington resigned his commission. He returned to Mount Vernon, which he had inherited a few years before, to settle back into civilian life. At twenty-six, he fell in love with and then married Martha Dandridge Custis, a wealthy young widow and mother of two children: John and Martha. He and Martha never had children of their own, but he raised his stepchildren as his own.

After spending most of his adult life serving his country on the battlefield, Washington turned his interest to politics. His hero status assured him an easy election to a seat in the Virginia House of Burgesses. After a few years, his leadership qualities, along with his unwavering loyalty to his constituents, earned him an unofficial position as leader of the Whigs, a group of dissenters to royal politics and their transatlantic interests. As a Whig, Washington took interest in most of the important local issues of the day, but in the early 1760s, one legal battle in particular captured his attention. It was a conflict between his neighbors and the Crown. The case became known as the *Parson's Cause*, and it put the Church of England at odds with the Virginia tobacco farmers. Patrick Henry, a brilliant young lawyer and orator, represented the farmers. The young man would become famous while handling that piece of litigation and used his newfound fame to launch his political career. He would eventually join Washington as a Whig in the Virginia House of Burgesses. Patrick Henry would be instrumental during the struggle for American independence.

Patrick Henry

The state of Virginia has erected a monument to its favorite sons: George Washington, Thomas Jefferson, and Patrick Henry. History has coined them, respectively, the Sword, the Pen, and the Trumpet of the American Revolution. To know and understand Patrick Henry is to know and understand the American Revolution. He was the very embodiment of American courage and patriotism. We recognize him today, as did his contemporaries, as the "Orator of Liberty." It was his eloquent and compelling speeches that motivated the hearts of the colonists to follow him into what seemed insurmountable odds to free themselves from British tyranny.

Henry was an unlikely revolutionary. He was a profound conservative and loathed any kind of radicalism that might erupt into violence. As a lawyer and part of the colonial gentry, he was devoted to conventional Whig principles: the rule of law, unswerving honor, and squire responsibilities. The early life of Henry gives no indication of his future greatness and notoriety. Born in 1736, Patrick Henry was reared in a devoutly Christian home in rural Virginia. As a child, he regularly attended church and sat under the masterful preaching of Reverend Samuel Davies, the prince of American preachers, arguably unequaled in the pulpits of that time. That early influence was probably the main ingredient in Henry's greatness as an orator and a spiritual leader.

Before studying law and subsequently starting his own law practice, Henry made several unsuccessful attempts to be in business for himself—a general store operator and later a tobacco farmer. With those failures came substantial debt, and it was that debt that motivated him to work hard and long in his law practice. In the first three years of his practice, Henry handled over eleven hundred cases and won most of them.

In 1763, while handling a controversial case known as the Parson's Cause, Henry's fame was born. In that case, he fought against taxation without representation in which Church of England parsons attempted to increase their tax on the colonists. The Anglican clerics were servants of the state, and therefore their salaries were to be collected by a government-enforced tithe. For the most part, the policy was begrudgingly accepted until late in the 1750s, when the plantation owners suffered a series of crop failures. The farmers had customarily paid their tax—or tithe—with a portion of their crops (sixteen thousand pounds of tobacco), but with sparse crops, it became difficult to meet their quota, so they elected to pay with Virginia's depreciated paper currency. The parsons, hoping to make a windfall on the much increased price of tobacco, sued for damages. In that David-versus-Goliath case, Henry was given little chance of winning, but with great determination and an eloquent argument, he stunned the jury and prevailed. Henry was then triumphantly carried out of the courthouse on the shoulders of the spectators. The Church of England had been defeated, and America's dissenting bias took flame.

With his new fame, Henry took up politics by winning a seat in the Virginia House of Burgesses, representing Louisa County. Within the first few days of accepting his seat, an important matter came up—England's infamous 1765 Stamp Act—which in effect raised taxes without representation. To Henry's dismay, the senior assemblymen appeared ready to accept the inevitability of that act without any opposition. At that time, it was not customary for junior assemblymen to be involved with debates, but instead to yield to the long-standing senior members. However, only nine days after accepting his seat, Henry, the junior assemblyman, submitted written resolutions in opposition to the Stamp Act. A "most bloody debate"[12] ensued against the entrenched aristocrats, an arena that favored Henry's great gift of oratory. Thomas Jefferson, an assemblyman in the

Burgess, described those orations: "They were great indeed, such as I have never heard from any other man."[12] In conclusion of the debate, Henry hurled defiance at King George III with a challenge, "If this be treason, make the most of it."[12]

Patrick Henry soon became the central figure in Virginia politics and the leading voice in the movement for independence and self-determination. During the second Virginia Convention in 1775, just after the British Navy had closed Boston Harbor, Henry delivered his most famous speech. His words became the trumpet that led the colonies into the Revolution. With great conviction, courage, and eloquence, he stated,

> Is life so dear, or peace so sweet, as to be purchased at the price of chains and slavery? Forbid it, Almighty God! I know not what course others may take, but as for me, give me liberty or give me death.[13]

The pinnacle of Henry's Virginia politics was reached when he became governor in 1776. He was subsequently elected for three additional consecutive terms (1777, 1778, and 1779). After a short leave from politics, Henry was reelected governor in 1784 and again the following year. He was also reelected in 1786, but he declined the honor.

The end of the Revolution did not mark the end of Henry's contribution to America. His greatest contribution was yet to come in the form of the Bill of Rights. As a protector of the sovereignty of the states, Henry took a stance with the anti-Federalists, who believed that the Constitution should speak the language of "We the States" instead of "We the People." While failing to stop the ratification of the Constitution, his arguments did raise awareness for the need of an enumerated list of rights guaranteed to the people. More than anyone else, Henry was responsible for the protection of basic civil liberties listed in the Bill of Rights. Liberty was not only Henry's passion, but also his legacy.

When Patrick Henry knew his life was near its end, he liquidated most of his real estate, which more than adequately provided for his wife and children. In his Last Will and Testament, he described what else he left them: "This is all the inheritance I give to my dear family, the religion of Christ will give one which will make them rich indeed."[14]

On June 6, 1799, Patrick Henry, with his tearful wife and children[g] all around him, took his last breath. His words of admonishment still trumpet today—we must not turn a deaf ear.

> It cannot be emphasized too strongly or too
> often that this great nation was founded, not by
> religionists, but by Christians;
> not on religion, but on the Gospel
> of Jesus Christ.
> For this very reason people of other faiths
> have been afforded asylum, prosperity, and freedom
> of worship here.[15]

* * *

> The great pillars of all government and of
> social life . . . [are] virtue, morality, and religion. This
> is the armor, my friend, and this alone, that renders
> us [America] invincible.[16]

---

[g] Patrick Henry had seventeen children: six children with his first wife, Sarah Shelton, who died in 1775, and eleven children with his second wife, Dorothy Spotswood. Patrick married Dorothy in 1777.

THE STAMP ACT CONGRESS

With the war for the domination of America finally over, King George III had to deal with the high cost of such a conquest, as well as the cost of maintaining control of his expanded empire. To deal with those problems, the king and the British Parliament unilaterally decided to send a portion of the Royal Army to America for its protection. The decision included passing on the cost of that protection to the colonies, along with part of Britain's war debt. The king further schemed to camouflage some additional recuperation of its war debt under the umbrella of the Stamp Act, a law that would require a stamp—for a fee—to be placed on every legal document, effectively levying a tax on all legal transactions. The colonies were unwilling to support such policies, because they felt that they were well able to protect themselves and because they recognized the Stamp Act for what is was—a tax. The fight was on!

While George Washington, Patrick Henry, and the other Whigs in the Virginia House of Burgesses were busy protesting those encroachments upon their liberty, other colonies joined their cause. However, the northern colonies protested from a slightly different perspective. The Virginia patriots had made the assertion that Parliament's Stamp Act had violated their basic inalienable (God-given) rights and their own independence, while many of the New England colonies maintained that as British subjects, they could not be taxed without their permission. "Taxation through representation" was a privilege that their transatlantic countrymen had enjoyed since Oliver Cromwell shattered the "divine right of kings" in the mid-seventeenth century.

In 1765, the Honorable James Otis, Esq., traveled all over Massachusetts, as well as other northern colonies, making speeches and stirring up opposition to the Crown's taxation policies. He asserted that the right for self-rule was God's gift to humanity. Therefore, no part of God's dominion could be taxed without the consent of the governed. He sent out a circular letter to the colonies proposing an ad hoc congress for the purpose of uniting in a common front against the parliamentary encroachments. That congress was held in New York on the first Tuesday of October and became known as the Stamp Act Congress. The twenty-seven delegates who attended the Stamp Act Congress are as follows:

- Massachusetts: James Otis, Oliver Partridge, and Timothy Ruggles

- New York: Robert R. Livingston, John Cruger, Philip Livingston, William Bayard, and Leonard Lispenard

- Connecticut: Eliphalet Dyer, David Rowland, and William Samuel Johnson

- The Pennsylvania counties of New Castle, Kent, and Sussex (which eventually became Delaware): Caesar Rodney and Thomas McKean

- Rhode Island: Metcalf Browler and Henry Ward

- Pennsylvania: George Bryan, John Morton, and John Dickenson

- New Jersey: Robert Ogden, Hendrick Fisher, and Joseph Borden

- South Carolina: Christopher Gadsden, John Rutledge, and Thomas Lynch

- Maryland: William Murdock, Edward Tilghman, and Thomas Ringold

The Virginia House of Burgesses chose not to send a delegation to the Stamp Act Congress.

Philip Livingston

Robert Livingston, the father of our subject, immigrated to America in the mid-1660s and settled in the Hudson River area. He came to New York from Scotland, where the Livingston name was highly esteemed and of exemplary character. In fact, his father was a well-known Scottish minister of the Gospel. Shortly after the death of his father, Robert, under the patroon privileges,[h] obtained a large tract of land that became known as the Livingston Manor.

Philip Livingston was born in Albany, New York, on January 15, 1716. Young Philip received a good Christian education that culminated at Yale College, from which he graduated with honors in 1737. He immediately thrust himself into commercial enterprises, often found in the middle of the most sophisticated business ventures in New York City. The honesty and integrity that he displayed during his dealings won him the trust and respect of the entire community.

In 1740, Philip married Christina Ten Broeck, the great-granddaughter of Dirck Wesselse Ten Broeck, who was named the first alderman of Albany in 1686. Over the next twenty-some years, Philip enjoyed the fruits of a

---

[h] Patroon Privilege was a Dutch land grant (or estate) that carried rights much like the English feudal system of lords and serfs. The grant was a perpetual inheritance and carried manorial rights.

prosperous life. His business grew and his family grew; nine children were born into their home.

In 1754, Philip Livingston was elected alderman of the East Ward of New York City,[i] a position he held for nine years in succession. As his interest in politics intensified, he shifted into the provincial government arena and became a member of the New York House of Representatives. During his tenure in the House, he was a recognized leader—so much so that he was chosen to be one of New York's delegates to the Stamp Act Congress. Upon his return in 1768, he was rewarded by being elevated to the position of Speaker of the Provincial House. Late the following year, in an attempt to quash the colony's rebellion, Governor Delancey dissolved the entire body of representatives.

When the Continental Congress was formed in 1774, Livingston was chosen as a delegate. He was on the committee that prepared the address to Parliament that outlined the colonies' grievances. Livingston remained an active member and, in 1776, he voted for and signed the Declaration of Independence. During the early part of the Revolutionary War, his house became the council of war meeting place for the colonial forces that were stationed at New York. It was at his house that Washington and his generals decided to retreat from Long Island, forcing Livingston's wife and children to flee from the city and live in exile until peace could be reached.

After independence was declared, the congressional delegates realized that the colonies had no governments of their own—only that which had been originally set up by the Crown. Therefore, each of the colonies immediately took steps to establish their state governments. To facilitate that transition in New York, a special convention was called for and Livingston was chosen as its president. The state government was soon created and, in 1777, Livingston was elected a senator in that new state legislature, a position he held until his death.

Early in 1778, Livingston—afflicted with dropsy in his chest and generally in poor health—requested leave from Congress so that he might return to his family to recover his health. His leave was granted, but it was cut short when Congress urgently summoned his return. Feeling a profound obligation to duty, he again took his seat in Congress. But before he left his

---

[i] The East Ward of New York City was a district that today encompasses the area of Wall Street.

home, knowing that he might well not return due to his poor health, he said a final good-bye to his family and friends. Three months later, the disease took his life. His son Henry, serving as aide to General Washington, was the only relative to see him before his death. Henry hurried to his father's bedside and stayed with him and comforted him until he passed away.

On June 12, 1778, at the age of sixty-two, the old patriot breathed his last breath. Although he was denied the satisfaction of seeing his country free from the despotic British rule, the name of Philip Livingston shall be forever remembered with great esteem.

John Morton

The ancestors of this patriot emigrated from Sweden to America during the early part of the seventeenth century and settled in the Delaware River area. The year 1724 was both the year that John Morton was born and the year that his father died. While John was yet an infant, his widowed mother married an English gentleman named John Sketchley, who became greatly attached to young John. Sketchley raised John as his own child and made sure that he acquired a good education. John excelled in mathematics, especially as it related to surveying, which, along with farming, became his chosen profession. Around 1745, John married Anne Justis, the daughter of a neighboring farmer who was also of Swedish descent. The Morton family eventually included three sons and five daughters.

Over the next few decades, John Morton became a pillar in his community, acquiring a great deal of wealth and the respect of his countrymen. He commenced his public career in 1764, when he was appointed justice of the peace. The following year, he was elected to the Provincial General Assembly, where his leadership skills were immediately recognized, and during his first year, he was chosen to attend James Otis's proposed Stamp Act Congress. When his work was complete on the national level, he returned to provincial politics where he was promoted to Speaker of the House, a station he held for many years. He also was honored with the position of high sheriff and then finally judge of the Pennsylvania Supreme Court, his last public office under British rule.

When England's oppression became intolerable and a move toward independence became imminent, Morton's leadership was once again sought on the national level. He was chosen as a delegate to attend the First Continental Congress. His presence stabilized its proceedings during the 1774, 1775, and 1776 sessions. When unanimous support was sought for that fateful July 4 vote for independence, the Pennsylvania coalition was locked in their decision—two votes for and two votes against. Morton was called upon officially to cast the deciding vote. With his affirmative vote, Pennsylvania stood with the other twelve colonies, unanimously voting for independence. In retrospect, Morton stated that it was "the most glorious service that [he] ever rendered [his] country."[17]

After independence was declared, he eagerly accepted the call of Congress to help frame the Articles of Confederation, a task he worked on tirelessly. John Morton literally worked himself to death. He was one of nine signers who never witnessed his country's freedom. He died in April 1777, after the labors of his responsibility had worn down his health. He was mourned by the citizens of Pennsylvania, who felt his leadership and patriotism were essential if they were to see their way through those turbulent times. He was buried at the St. James Church, where he and his family had attended regularly. Insight as to what would possess a man to give his all to the cause of American freedom, as John Morton did, may be found in an excerpt from his Last Will and Testament: "With an awful reverence to the Great Almighty God, Creator of all mankind, being sick and weak in body but of sound mind and memory, thanks be given to Almighty God for the same."[18] John Morton believed that the colonial cause was a righteous one.

John Dickenson

In a rural section of Talbot County, Maryland, near the village of Trappe, John Dickenson,[j] who has been called the "penman of the Revolution," was born. The year was 1732, and the setting was Crosiadore Estate, a plantation owned by his parents, Samuel and Mary Dickenson. When John was eight years of age, his family relocated to Kent County, Pennsylvania (which eventually became part of Delaware) where private tutors saw to his early education. In 1750, he moved to Philadelphia and began the study of law, later transferring to London's Middle Temple[k] where, four years later, he put the finishing polish on his studies. He returned to Philadelphia and soon established himself as a prominent lawyer and one of the most

---

[j] In some documents, Dickenson is spelled with an "i" instead of his usual "e" (Dickinson).

[k] The Inn of Court was an institution for teaching law and was first established in London by the Knights of Templar during the reign of Henry II (twelfth century). Eventually, two more colleges of law were added, making three in total: the Inner, Middle, and Outer Temples. The Middle Inn was added during the reign of Edward III (thirteenth century), and the Outer Temple was added during the reign of Elizabeth (sixteenth century).

sought-after bachelors in the province. In 1770, he married Miss Mary "Polly" Norris, a local socialite, and began a family. John and Polly had five children, but only three reached maturity.

In 1760, just three years after John's return from England, his reputation had earned him a seat in the Assembly of the Three Lower Counties,[1] where he soon became the speaker. Two years later, he was elected to the Philadelphia seat in the Pennsylvania General Assembly, an office he held until 1764. Being a devout Quaker, he opposed any kind of open rebellious behavior against the Royal authority—a stance that tarnished his reputation with some of his constituents. As a result, he lost his seat in the General Assembly. However, he used every legal means at his disposal to fight the Stamp Act. He turned to his pen and authored "The Late Regulations Respecting the British Colonies on the Continent of America Considered . . ." an influential pamphlet that earned him notoriety throughout the colonies. In his writings, he stated, "The rights essential to happiness . . . We claim them from a higher source—from the King of Kings, and Lord of all the earth. They are not annexed to us by parchments and seals."[19] Through the power of his pen, he was appointed a delegate to the Stamp Act Congress, and subsequently, he drafted its resolutions.

When the British Parliament repealed the Stamp Act, joy was everywhere in the colonies, but the elation was short lived because the king made it clear that he was not about to give up on his intention to tax his American colonies. Over the next few years, Parliament introduced a series of obtrusive bills such as the Townshend Act, all with the intent of camouflaging taxation. In response, Dickenson put his pen back to work. He authored a series of articles for the *Pennsylvania Chronicles*, "Letters from a Farmer in Pennsylvania," in which he popularized the theory of counteracting the British aggression with the use of non-importation and non-exportation agreements. His theories were widely embraced, and it became vogue to buy American products even though, in many instances, they were more expensive and of lesser quality. These embargos put Britain's economy into a tailspin. His fame grew, and he received thanks from every corner of America. Princeton University awarded him an honorary degree in theology.

---

[1] The three counties — New Castle, Kent, Sussex — eventually became the state of Delaware in 1776.

Dickenson was reluctantly drawn into the revolutionary movement when he agreed to chair Philadelphia's Committee of Correspondence in 1774. That same year he was elected to the Continental Congress, but resigned in 1776 due to his opposition to the Declaration of Independence. His opposition was based only on the assumption that it might be premature. On the floor of Congress, just before the Declaration was voted on, Dickenson eloquently and solemnly invoked the "Governor of the Universe" to convince the minds of the other members that if independence was God's will, nothing he would say would make the least impression. He then proceeded to make his arguments against independence. His arguments—though eloquent and logical—failed to resonate with the majority.

In 1779 and 1780, he again took a seat in the Continental Congress, where his most significant accomplishment was signing the Articles of Confederation. In 1782, he was elected governor of Pennsylvania, a position he held for three years. Several years later, he attended the Annapolis Convention, an assembly whose purpose it was to amend the Articles of Confederation. During that convention, it became apparent that mere amendments were not sufficient, so the call was made for a Constitutional Convention. Although he was chosen as a delegate to that convention, he had limited involvement due to his poor health. In fact, he authorized his friend and fellow delegate, George Read, to sign for him in his absence.

The Constitutional Convention closed out John Dickenson's public life, but he remained active for two more decades, writing on various political topics and publishing a collection of his work in 1801. John Dickenson, who died in 1808 at the age of seventy-five, made the following statement in his Last Will and Testament:

> Rendering thanks to my Creator for my existence and station among His works, for my birth in a country enlightened by the Gospel and enjoying freedom, and for all His other kindnesses, to Him I resign myself, humbly confiding in His goodness and in His mercy through Jesus for the events of eternity.[20]

Northern Dissent
to the Crown

George Washington
1764 – 1769

Throughout the 1760s, George Washington was enjoying his domestic life and was dividing his time between his political pursuits and the managerial demands of a large plantation. In 1760, he expanded his civic responsibilities and began serving as a judge in the county of his residence, an office he held for fourteen years. In his two public offices, the House of Burgesses and on the bench, he established a good reputation and gained considerable knowledge in the science of civil government.

With the Stamp Act repealed and tranquility restored between the mother country and her American colonies, Great Britain would have been wise to cease her desire to control and tax her offspring. If she had, the historical significance of George Washington's life and career may have ended here—except maybe a final footnote stating that he died at age sixty-eight after maintaining a life of excellent character, making impartial judicial decisions from the bench, performing wise and dutiful civil service, and being fully devoted to his church and family. However, Providence held a very different destiny for George Washington.

During that time, Great Britain did not possess much wisdom at its helm. A short time after the Stamp Act had been repealed, Britain's imbecile Treasury Secretary, Charles Townshend, addressed Parliament: "Fear! Cowards! Dare not tax America! . . . I [will] dare to tax America!" And tax he did. In June 1767, the Townshend Acts was enacted, imposing stiff tariffs, levies, and duties on the colonies. The act further stipulated that violators would be arrested and prosecuted in court—however, not by a jury of their peers, but by judges appointed by the Crown and paid through their collections. In October 1768, as political tensions intensified, Great Britain posted a standing army in many of the colonies.

During those exasperating times, the North became the main theater of dissent against Royal tyranny. Most of the dissenting speech and anti-Crown demonstrations were delivered and coordinated through patriots like James Otis and Samuel Adams, both of whom had achieved national fame while protesting the Stamp Act. For Otis's opposition and dissenting speech, he would pay a high price—he was targeted for assassination by a group of Royal soldiers stationed in Boston.

During the late 1760s, the American colonies continued to unite and also began to prepare themselves for self-government, much of which was accomplished under the renowned instruction of John Witherspoon, who has been called the "Father of the Founding Fathers." Washington made Witherspoon's acquaintance during a visit to Congress in 1776.

James Otis

James Otis, a pioneer of patriots, was born on February 5, 1725, at West Barnstable, Massachusetts. He was the namesake of his father, Colonel James Otis, Sr., who had distinguished himself as an officer in the state militia. Colonel Otis was also a prominent lawyer and an influential statesman in provincial politics. Being an elite member of Boston's high society, Colonel Otis paid close attention to the preparatory studies of young James. That special attention led to large dividends when James graduated from Harvard College in 1743, at only eighteen years of age. He was admitted to the bar five years later and, in 1750, founded a law practice in Boston.

In 1755, James Otis met, courted, and married "the beautiful Ruth Cunningham," the daughter of a successful merchant and the heiress to the Cunningham fortune. Although they seemed to be made for each other, their politics were very different—at opposite ends of the political spectrum. Ruth was described by James as being a "High Tory" and far too good for him. However, their political differences did not seem to inhibit the growth of their family, which eventually included three children—two daughters and one son.[m]

With his professionalism, legal ingenuity, and oratory talents, Otis's law practice flourished and landed him a government post as sole judge of the Massachusetts Court of Admiralty. That court had charge of the navigation laws, which included the responsibility of controlling all forms of smuggling. Parliament granted his court extended search-and-seizure privileges under writs of assistance, whereby officers could enter peoples' homes, ships, or stores at any time in search of contraband. These writs differed from search warrants in that no probable cause was required. In 1761, James Otis sacrificed his reputation and professional career when he resigned his position rather than enforce such tyrannical polices. Prior to resigning, he argued before the superior court for three hours, raising the doctrine of natural law (laws of Nature and God) and stated, "A man who is quiet and orderly is as secure in his house as a prince in his castle." During his oration, he laid the foundational arguments that patriots would draw upon for years to come. He coined the phrase "Taxation without representation." John Adams, who was in attendance, described him and his orations as "a flame of fire, the seeds of patriots and heroes were then and there sown."

Otis published his arguments in a pamphlet, titled *The Rights of the British Colonies Asserted and Proved*, thus severing any political ties with the Crown. He then joined Samuel Adams in a leadership position with the opposition party after being elected to the provincial legislature. Otis's brilliant oratory became the inspiration that led Adams to mobilize the Sons of Liberty, which became the organizational hub of the northern resistance to the Crown prior to the Revolution.

When the Stamp Act was introduced, Otis first called for the Stamp Act Congress, an action that bolstered his Whig credentials. In 1766, he was

---

[m] The names of James Otis's three children were James, Elizabeth and Mary. James died before reaching the age of twenty. The girls matured and eventually became as politically diverse as their parents. Mary, the elder of the two, became a Loyalist like her mother and married a captain in the British Army. At the conclusion of the War of Independence, Mary and Captain Brown took up their lives in London, where she remained for the rest of her life. Elizabeth took after her father and became a staunch Whig and eventually married Benjamin Lincoln, the son—and namesake—of one of Washington's favorite generals.

chosen Speaker of the House, and throughout America, patriots sought his opinion and advice. In fact, the following year, even the highly respected John Dickenson sent him the first of his "Farmer" letters to get his "opinion . . . [and to] determine its true worth." By 1769, James Otis had become the unofficial political leader of New England and was described as a "malignant incendiary" by many British public officials.

On September 5, 1769, after one of his "treasonous" articles appeared in the *Boston Gazette*, Otis was brutally assaulted by a gang of British soldiers while he was eating in a public dining room. After extinguishing the lights, one of the assassins drew his sword and viciously wheeled it at the defenseless Otis, splitting open his head. Leaving him for dead, the Royal butchers quickly made their way through the crowd that had begun to assemble, escaping to the refuge of one of the king's ships that was docked in the harbor. They were eventually tried for attempted murder and fined five thousand pounds sterling in damages—a small price to pay for effectively snuffing out the useful life of one of America's most influential early patriots.

James Otis never recovered. He was left with permanent brain damage that caused fits of rage, leading the courts to declare him mentally insane. He made a partial recovery in 1775 and volunteered to fight at the Battle of Bunker Hill, but his seizures returned, forcing him to retire to his home, where he remained until his death. His sister, Mercy Otis Warren,[n] described Otis's last years—and eventual death—as follows:

> Mr. Otis lived to see the independence of America, though in a state of mind incapable of enjoying fully the glorious event which his own exertions had precipitated. After several years of mental derangement, as if in consequence of his own prayers, his great soul was instantly set free by a flash of lightning, from the evils in which the love of his country had involved him.

---

[n] Mercy Otis Warren (1728–1814), the sister of James Otis and wife of Joseph Warren (president of the Massachusetts Provincial Congress), was perhaps the most formidable female intellectual in eighteenth-century America. She wrote *History of the Rise, Progress, and Termination of the American Revolution*, a comprehensive study of the events of the American Revolution and the establishment of the post-Confederation government.

His death took place in May, one thousand seven hundred and eighty three, the same year the peace was concluded between Great Britain and America.[21]

James Otis not only influenced patriots from every corner of America, but he also played a major role in shaping the lives of his siblings. His sister Mercy, his brother Joseph, and his youngest brother, Samuel, all became leaders in America's struggle for freedom. One of James Otis's most influential pamphlets was the *The Rights of the British Colonies Asserted and Proved*, and in that publication, he set the stage for the revolutionary cause being on a righteous foundation:

> Has [government] any solid foundation? Any chief corner stone? . . . I think it has an everlasting foundation in the unchangeable will of God . . . The sum of my arguments is that civil government is of God.[22]

John Witherspoon

Late one August night in 1768, a crowd of people, many of whom were dignitaries, assembled at Princeton, New Jersey, anxiously awaiting the arrival of the acclaimed reverend John Witherspoon. The attendees had traveled from as far away as Philadelphia and New York City, each one hoping to meet the man who many believed would galvanize the fragmented American colonies. Nassau Hall was lit with candles in his honor, and when John Witherspoon finally graced them with his presence, the elated crowd broke into a chorus of cheers.

True to his reputation, Witherspoon became one of the most influential figures in the founding of America and has been called the Father of the Founding Fathers. At Princeton University, under his direct instruction, he helped train America's first generation of leaders, including one president, one vice president, twelve governors, three Supreme Court justices, twenty-one senators, thirty-nine congressmen, and ten cabinet members—eighty-seven Founding Fathers in total. He taught two basic components of American patriotism and identified its primary enemy:

That he is the best friend to American liberty [first] who is the most sincere and active in promoting true and undefiled religion, and [second] who sets himself with the greatest firmness to bear down profanity and immorality of every kind. Whoever is an avowed enemy of God, I scruple not to call him an enemy to his country.[23]

John Witherspoon was born in Edinburgh, Scotland in 1723. He was the son of a Gospel minister and a direct descendant of the great Reformer, John Knox. With that godly heritage, it is not surprising that young John was destined for the ministry. In 1736, at fourteen, having completed his preparatory education, he was enrolled in the University of Edinburgh. He especially excelled in sacred literature and graduated with his theology degree. His education continued at the University of St. Andrews, where he earned his doctorate of divinity. At twenty-one, he became a licensed preacher.

In 1744, Reverend Witherspoon accepted the parsonage of Beith in the west of Scotland. He unselfishly ministered there for twenty-two years, despite being offered at least three different, more prominent parishes. At the time of his appointment, he had just married Elizabeth Montgomery, a woman whose piety, benevolence, and graciousness endeared her to all who knew her. He and Mrs. Witherspoon had ten children.

By the mid-1760s, Reverend Witherspoon had published three doctrinal sermons in which he lashed out against religious decadence and taught defiance to ecclesiastic authorities in the paganized church hierarchy. His writings gained him international stature and employment offers from churches in Ireland, Holland, and America. The American offer came from Princeton University, which had been founded in 1746 and was renowned for its spiritual heritage—student requirements included daily worship, attendance at church on the Sabbath, and religious instruction.

In 1766, the board of governors of Princeton University offered Dr. Witherspoon the presidency. The opportunity would give him a new and enlarged platform for his ministry, his political philosophy, and his powers of persuasion. He would be able to influence American religious circles, education, and the political system. He first graciously refused the invitation, but after personal visits from Richard Stockton and Dr. Benjamin Rush—both Princeton graduates—he accepted the position.

Princeton University graduated about twenty students per year, so Reverend Witherspoon was able to personally tutor every pupil. He changed the curriculum to include subjects such as political science, debate, and oratory, insisting that all graduates be prepared for holding public office. He taught that rebellion against despots is obedience to God. He also taught that God is supreme, and therefore His law transcends any earthly political order (His laws are inalienable). His teachings were not meant to hurt Great Britain, but instead to defend American privileges. However, the English labeled Princeton the "seminary of sedition," as it was the scene of many anti Great Britain student demonstrations. Under the leadership of Witherspoon, Princeton University grew in both intellectual and financial stature and quickly became eminent among American higher learning institutions.

As British aggression escalated, Witherspoon's influence expanded to the political arena. In 1774, he published a prophetic essay in which he predicted the path that Congress ultimately took in the American Revolution. He believed that America would remain loyal to the Crown unless it was forced into disloyalty by self-defense. In 1775, he became a member of the Committee of Correspondence and, in 1776, a member of the New Jersey Provincial Congress, as well as a delegate to the Continental Congress. During the debate for independence, one delegate° remarked that "the people are not ripe for a Declaration of Independence." Witherspoon replied, "In my judgment, Sir, the country is not only ripe for independence, but we are in danger of becoming rotten for the want of it, if we delay any longer."[24] Needless to say, he gladly voted for and signed that glorious document. He remained active in Congress throughout the revolutionary period and served on over one hundred different committees.

When the war with Great Britain broke out, Witherspoon admonished the Continental troops to set themselves apart from cursing and drunkenness and all other immoral behavior, and instead to reverence the name of the Lord and walk in his precepts. His reasoning for these admonitions was that "there is no soldier so undaunted as the pious man, no army so formidable as those who are superior to the fear of death."[25] The Reverend lost two of his sons on the battlefield of the American Revolution.

° John Dickenson was that dissenting delegate.

When peace was reached, he retired from Congress and concentrated on the rebuilding of Princeton. He also remained involved with state politics as a member of the New Jersey Assembly until 1787. In 1789, he served as a member of the State Ratification Convention for the federal Constitution.

From 1790 until his death in 1794, he was completely dedicated to his ministerial duties. He was undaunted in his ministry, regularly delivering his message from the pulpit, notwithstanding the loss of his eyesight two years before his death. After his death, John Adams said of him, "A true son of liberty. So he was. But first, he was a son of the Cross."[26] He declared in his Last Will and Testament,

> I shall now conclude my discourse by preaching this Savior to all who hear me, and entreating you in the most earnest manner to believe in Jesus Christ, for "there is no salvation in any other" [Acts 4:12] . . . If you are not reconciled to God through Jesus Christ, if you are not clothed with the spotless robe of His righteousness, you must forever perish.[27]

A reverend and a statesman, John Witherspoon had many strong views that were relevant at our nation's founding, and some that are still relevant today, as these found among his many writings prove. On slavery:

> It is certainly unlawful to make inroads upon others . . . and take away their liberty by no other better means than superior power.[28]

On moral character of our elected officials:

> The people in general ought to have regard to the moral character of those whom they invest with authority either in the legislature, executive, or judicial branches.[29]

A democratic versus republican form of government:

> Pure democracy cannot subsist long nor be carried far into the departments of state—it is very subject to caprice [impulse] and the madness of popular rage.[30]

On Christianity versus other religions:

> The Christian religion is superior to every other . . . But there is not only an excellence in the Christian morals, but a manifest superiority in them to those which are derived from any other source.[31]

On separation of church and state:

> To promote true religion is the best and most effective way of making a virtuous and regular people. Love to God and love to man is the substance of religion; when these prevail, civil laws will have little to do . . . Those who are vested with civil authority ought to promote religion and good morals among all under their government.[32]

THE BOSTON MASSACRE
AND BOSTON TEA PARTY

The violence in Boston did not end with the assault on James Otis—it began with it. In the following year, 1770, the city once again witnessed the brutality of the British during the horrific episode known as the Boston Massacre—an atrocity that ushered in many years of bitterness and turmoil between the Bostonians and the Crown. The infamous Boston Tea Party in 1773 marked the peak of their dissidence and provoked the British Parliament to retaliate and pass the Intolerable Acts, which effectively closed the Boston port. Samuel Adams immediately called on the other colonies for aid.

Upon receiving Adams's plea for aid, the Virginia Assembly flew into action. On June 1, 1774, the day the Port Act (the closing of Boston Harbor) was to take effect, George Washington's friend and fellow patriot, Thomas Jefferson, drafted a resolution calling for a "day of fasting and prayer." He asked all people of America to "invoke the divine interposition [that they might become] one heart and one mind"[33] to oppose the British aggression.

As a result, supplies poured into Massachusetts, not just from Virginia, but from all over America. As an initial contributor, Washington personally donated fifty pounds sterling (today's equivalency is $10,000) to the cause. Along with aid from Connecticut came a letter drafted by Israel Putnam, telling the people of Boston, "You are held up as a spectacle to the whole world. All Christendom is longing to see the event of the American contest."[33] With thankful hearts, the people of Boston responded with a circular letter, dated August 22, 1774:

> The Christian sympathy and generosity of our friends through the continent cannot fail to inspire the inhabitants of this town with patience, resignation and firmness, while we trust in the Supreme Ruler of the universe, that He will graciously hear our cries, and in His time free us from our present bondage, and make us rejoice in His great salvation.[34]

A few weeks later, delegates from twelve of the thirteen colonies met in Philadelphia to participate in the First Continental Congress (the colony of Georgia did not attend).

Samuel Adams

Samuel Adams, the father of the American Revolution, was born in Boston on September 22, 1722. Samuel's father, a man of influence and means, served in the Massachusetts Assembly, owned a profitable malting business, and lived in a mansion on Purchase Street that provided a spectacular view of Boston Harbor. Young Samuel was well educated, graduating from Harvard when he was only eighteen years old. For his career, Samuel entered the mercantile business arena as an apprentice with Thomas Cushing, a prominent Boston merchant. However, the business did not hold much appeal for Samuel, whose real interest seemed to lie in politics. Even though his father had supplied Samuel with ample investment capital to launch his own mercantile business, his political distractions prevented him from making a success of it.

When his father died in 1747, Samuel inherited the malting business and a substantial amount of cash. Two years later, he married Elizabeth Checkley, the daughter of Reverend Samuel Checkley, pastor of the South Church of Boston. They had five children before Elizabeth died in 1757.

With the death of his father, Samuel Adams became even more submerged in all the political issues of the day. He wrote seditious columns for the newspaper (often under pen names), debated at town hall meetings, and in general, stirred up the colonies against the British government. Meanwhile, Adams's business suffered from mismanagement and poor investments. As a result, he took a job as a tax collector. Under his administration, tax collections suffered terribly because Adams refused to collect (by taking a pig or the last bit of grain) from people who could not afford to pay. He told his supervisor that "the town didn't need the taxes as badly as the poor people needed to keep their belongings and that he would rather lose his job than force such collections."[35] Regarding his second cousin's personal ambitions, John Adams said, "My Brother,[P] Samuel Adams, says he never looked forward in his life; never planned, laid a scheme or formed a design of laying up anything for himself or others after him."[36] The citizens of Boston came to love and respect him and would have elected him to any political office.

With his family suffering from the same neglect that doomed his business, Samuel Adams married Elizabeth Wells. The happy event occurred in 1764. Thirteen years his junior, Elizabeth was an able stepmother who managed the household skillfully.

In 1765, Adams was chosen as a representative for Boston in the General Assembly. He became distinguished for his intelligence, his enthusiasm, and his leadership in the opposition to the Crown. His influence was so recognized and respected that Governor Thomas Gage tried to buy his silence, once offering him a substantial bribe if he would just cease his hostilities toward the Royal government. Samuel Adams refused, stating, "I trust I have long since made my peace with the King of Kings. No personal consideration shall induce me to abandon the righteous cause of my country."[37] In the years to come, that firm stance and other similar actions caused Governor Gage to withhold from Adams his offer to pardon all who would reaffirm their allegiance to Britain. John Hancock was the only other Whig crusader not to be included in the governor's offer to pardon. In fact, Governor Gage later gave the orders to "hang them on the spot" should they be captured.

On March 5, 1770, less than a year after the attempted assassination of James Otis (Samuel Adams's mentor), another act of British violence stunned the citizens of Boston. A group of young people, who had gathered

---

[P] Both cousins—John Adams and Samuel Adams—always referred to each other as brothers.

in the streets and were outraged by the presence of British soldiers, began to throw snowballs at the redcoats. The two groups began shouting at each other, but those actions soon escalated into a scuffle, and then seconds later, the impetuous soldiers fired shots. When the smoke cleared, three of the young townspeople lay dead and two others fatally wounded. Adams exploited that event to the fullest extent, coining it the Boston Massacre. Fearing a revolt, the governor ordered the standing army to leave Boston, which for a while restored some calm.

In 1772, along with Richard Henry Lee of Virginia, Samuel Adams proposed to organize the Committees of Correspondence, which united the colonies into one voice and synchronized their efforts. Later that same year, he wrote *The Rights of the Colonists* in an attempt to educate the people about their violated rights. In it, he stated the following:

> The Rights of the Colonists as Christians. These may be best understood by reading and carefully studying the institutes of the great Law Giver and Head of the Christian Church, which are to be found and promulgated in the New Testament.[38]

In that pamphlet, he suggested that the colonists could read the Bible and discover for themselves that their "God-given" or "inalienable rights" had been violated by Great Britain.

On December 16, 1773, Samuel Adams delivered a fomenting speech to a group of his disciples, known as the Sons of Liberty. After that speech—which protested the British duty that had been placed upon the tea that was imported by the colonies—Adams and the other patriots disguised themselves as Indians, went down to the port, boarded three British ships in Boston Harbor, and dumped fifteen thousand pounds of tea overboard. That act became known as the Boston Tea Party. Parliament retaliated by issuing the Intolerable Acts, which included closing Boston Harbor (to starve the citizens into submission), quartering troops in civilian homes, and appointing Crown judges (rather than judges elected by the people).

Samuel Adams immediately put the Committees of Correspondence to work, sending out a circular to all the colonies explaining Boston's predicament and requesting aid. Their countrymen responded without hesitation, and in no time supplies were pouring into Boston. Later, he employed the same network to call for the First Continental Congress, which also had a favorable response.

On September 5, 1774, Adams attended that First Continental Congress where he, not surprisingly, became one of the most active members. In 1776, once the Declaration of Independence had been signed, he declared, "We have this day restored the Sovereign to Whom all men ought to be obedient. He reigns in heaven and from the rising to the setting of the sun let His Kingdom come."[39] He retired from Congress in 1781 after he completed his work on the Articles of Confederation.

In 1788, Samuel Adams emerged again in politics, on the state level. He served as a member of the state convention for the ratification of the federal Constitution. In 1789, he became the lieutenant governor of Massachusetts, an office he held until 1794, when he was elected governor. He retired from the governorship in 1797 at age seventy-five. Samuel Adams died on October 3, 1803. He declared the following in his Last Will and Testament: "Principally, and first of all, I resign my soul to the Almighty Being who gave it, and my body I commit to the dust, relying on the merits of Jesus Christ for the pardon of my sins."[40]

Samuel Adams's life is a shining example of a true patriot. He was undaunted in his belief that America would be successful in its struggle for freedom because he believed its motives were righteous and that God was on America's side. In a letter to some British officials, he declared that belief:

There is One above us who will take exemplary vengeance for every insult upon His majesty. You know that the cause of America is just. You know that she contends for that freedom to which all men are entitled—that she contends against oppression, rapine, and more than savage barbarity. The blood of the innocent is upon your hands, and all the waters of the ocean will not wash it away. We again make our solemn appeal to the God of Heaven to decide between you and us. And we pray that, in the doubtful scale of battle, we may be successful as we have justice on our side, and that the merciful Savior of the world may forgive our oppressors.[41]

In the manifesto for the Continental Congress, he reflected a similar tone:

> We, therefore, the Congress of the United States of America, do solemnly declare and proclaim that . . . we appeal to God who searcheth the hearts of men for the rectitude of our intentions; and in His holy presence declare that, as we are not moved by any light or hasty suggestions of anger or revenge, so through every possible change or fortune we will adhere to this our determination.[42]

PART II

The Cast Is Chosen

THE FIRST
CONTINENTAL CONGRESS

With Samuel Adams's call for a Continental Congress almost unanimously accepted, delegates began arriving at Carpenters' Hall in Philadelphia on September 5, 1774. Each colony chose its most trusted and able citizens to represent its interest in the new body. The Virginia contingent included Peyton Randolph, Richard Henry Lee, George Washington, Patrick Henry, and Benjamin Harrison—men who would have done honor to any age or country.

Once the delegates were gathered, the meeting opened with prayer. To administer the invocation, Samuel Adams chose Reverend Jacob Duché. He was Episcopalian, and Adams thought Duché might help cement the support of the Episcopalians from Virginia. In a letter to his wife, John Adams described the proceedings as follows:

> [Reverend Duché] read several prayers . . . and then read the thirty-fifth Psalm. You must remember, this was the next morning after we heard the horrible rumor of the cannonade of Boston. I never saw a greater effect upon an audience. It seemed as if Heaven had ordained that Psalm to be read on that morning . . . I must beg you to read the Psalm.[1]

Psalm 35 reads:

> Plead my cause, O Lord, with them that strive with me: fight against them that fight against me. Take hold of shield and buckler, and stand up for mine help. Draw out also the spear, and stop the way against them that persecute me: say unto my soul, I am thy salvation. Let them be confounded and put to shame that seek after my soul; let them be as chaff before the wind: and let the angel of the Lord chase them. Let their way be dark and slippery: and let the angel of the Lord persecute them. For without cause have they hid from me their net in a pit, which without cause they digged for my soul . . .

Silas Deane (a Connecticut delegate) noted the following:

> Washington was kneeling there, and Henry, and Randolph, and Rutledge, and Lee and Jay; and by their side there stood, bowed down in deference, the Puritan Patriots of New England, who at that moment had reason to believe that an armed soldiery was wasting their humble households . . . They prayed fervently for "America, for the Congress, for the province of Massachusetts Bay, and especially for the town of Boston." Who can realize the emotions with which they turned imploringly to heaven for divine interposition and aid? "It was enough," said Mr. Adams, "to melt a heart of stone. I saw the tears gush into the eyes of the old pacific Quakers of Philadelphia."[2]

Several hours after Reverend Duché had begun the invocation and Bible study, the delegates began their business, feeling reassured that the Governor of the Universe would direct them. The delegates then unanimously elected Peyton Randolph to be the president of the Continental Congress.

The names of the delegates who attended the First Continental Congress are as follows:

- New Hampshire: John Sullivan, Nathaniel Folsom

- Massachusetts Bay: Thomas Cushing, Samuel Adams, John Adams, Robert Treat Paine, and John Hancock

- Rhode Island: Stephen Hopkins and Samuel Ward

- Connecticut: Eliphalet Dyer, Roger Sherman, and Silas Deane

- New York: Isaac Low, John Alsop, John Jay, James Duane, William Floyd, Henry Weisner, and Samuel Bocrum

- New Jersey: James Kinsey, William Livingston, Stephen Crane, and Richard Smith

- Pennsylvania: Joseph Galloway, Charles Humphreys, John Dickenson, Thomas Mifflin, Edward Biddle, John Morton, and George Ross

- Delaware: Caesar Rodney, George Read, and Thomas McKean

- Maryland: Matthew Tilghman, Thomas Johnson, William Paca, Samuel Chase, and Robert Goldsborough

- Virginia: Richard Henry Lee, George Washington, Patrick Henry, Richard Bland, Jr., Benjamin Harrison, Edmund Pendleton, and Peyton Randolph

- North Carolina: William Hooper, Joseph Hewes, and Richard Caswell

- South Carolina: Henry Middleton, Thomas Lynch, Christopher Gadsden, John Rutledge, and Edward Rutledge

Peyton Randolph

A rriving in the early 1600s, the Randolph family was among Virginia's first colonists. The later generations boasted of having the royal blood of Powhatan, the father of Pocahontas and emperor of the Powhatan Confederation (a group of over twenty Indian tribes in the vicinity of the Potomac River), in their veins.

Peyton Randolph was born in Williamsburg, Virginia in 1721. As a child, he embraced his studies, and at age thirteen, in an attempt to attain a more refined and complete education, he began a self-guided study of the classics.[q] Having the reputation of a scholar, he entered his hometown College of William and Mary[r] where he graduated with honors. As a high-profile alumnus, he tutored many of the most able men of the

---

[q] A "classical" education included learning Greek and Latin fluently (and Hebrew for theological studies) so that the students could read and study the classic authors (historians, poets, and philosophers) in their own language. A classical education was considered a broad-based education.

[r] College of William and Mary was founded in 1692 by Reverend James Blair, and it was his desire that the youth may be piously enacted in good letters and manners and that "the Christian faith may be propagated . . . to the glory of Almighty God." A century later, it was still pursuing this excellence with mandatory prayer times and public worship in the college chapel. The curriculum provided the moral foundation that was so essential for the future revolutionary era.

South—including Patrick Henry—and became a mentor to many up-and-coming statesmen. Peyton then sailed for England and continued his law studies at the Inner Temple in London. Upon completion, he returned home and in 1744 became a member of the Virginia bar. A year later, with his career on the fast track, he decided to redirect some of his efforts toward the development of his domestic life. His efforts proved successful and, in the spring of 1746, Peyton Randolph married Miss Elizabeth Harrison. Married life did not impede Randolph's career advancements in any way. By 1748, he had gained such a reputation among his peers that the Crown appointed him as the king's attorney of Virginia.

The same year that Randolph became attorney general, he also was elected to Virginia's House of Burgesses, where he served faithfully for the remainder of his life. He also served as a commander in the colonial militia. In 1756, during the height of the French and Indian War, he collected a regiment of one hundred men and led them into the interior, where he successfully completed several campaigns before returning to politics. As he became a landmark in the provincial government, his elegant home in Williamsburg became the site of most of the after-hours political meetings. He saw himself as a spokesman for Virginia politics, which included the views of both the Tories and the Whigs. Although he was opposed to the radical response that the colonists had toward the Stamp Act, his patriotism was never in question. As the British aggression increased, his Whig colors began to show and, in 1773, his peers elevated him to chairman of Virginia's Committee of Correspondence.

The following year, when Virginia sent its seven delegates to Philadelphia for the first session of the Continental Congress, Randolph was the natural leader. Once there, he was unanimously chosen as president of the convocation. From that point on, the term "president" always was used in conjunction with the highest office in the United States. The delegates entered into business, hearts bursting with patriotism and a sense of common and equal rights. First, Congress decided that even though the more populated colonies had more delegates present, each colony would cast only one vote. As a body, they resolved to cautiously avoid everything that might widen the breach between them and their mother country. They were determined not to submit to the chains of slavery that Parliament was advocating and, at the same time, they would prepare for a vigorous resistance, if necessary.

After much discussion, the delegates decided that Congress should formally petition the king by way of a list of grievances and violated rights, followed by a request for redress. In the petition Congress said,

> We ask but for peace, liberty and safety. We wish not a diminution of the prerogative, nor do we solicit the grant of any new rights in our favour. Your authority over us, and our connexion with Great Britain, we shall always carefully and zealously endeavor to support and maintain.[3]

The petition was signed by each delegate and then sent off to England. Congress further resolved to enter into non-importation, non-consumption, and non-exportation agreements, as well as to prepare an address to the people of Great Britain and another to the people of Canada. Those addresses can be summed up in the following words: "Place us in the same situation that we were, at the close of the last war [French and Indian], and our former harmony will be restored."[4] With that business completed, Congress was sent home and agreed to meet again on May 10, 1775, or sooner, should Parliament respond.

Five days prior to the October 26, 1774 recess of Congress, Randolph was forced to take leave due to poor health. During his absence, Henry Middleton[5] filled his seat, serving as the second president of Congress. The following spring, Randolph returned to Philadelphia as president of Congress, but only for a few days before suffering a stroke. John Hancock was then unanimously voted to fill the vacancy.

Peyton Randolph died on October 22, 1775, never living to see America's independence. Though his time on the national front was short, his leadership was essential to that First Continental Congress, and his elevated position there served as the highlight of his illustrious life, which he had dedicated to public service. For that dedication, he is remembered among the most revered and beloved founders of the United States of America.

---

[5] For a brief biography of Henry Middleton, see Arthur Middleton's biography in Part III.

Charles Thomson

Having just elected its first president, Peyton Randolph, the First Continental Congress then determined that it needed a competent secretary, someone who could keep the official minutes for all of its proceedings. President Randolph knew just the man: Charles Thomson. Randolph and Thomson were related through marriage; both of their wives were products of the Harrison dynasty in Virginia, a well-connected and politically minded family. Congress immediately dispatched a messenger to beckon Charles Thomson to duty. Thomson answered the call and became Congress's secretary on September 10, 1774—just five days after Congress had convened, but before all the delegates had taken their chairs. He served diligently in that capacity until 1788 when the system of government changed under the newly adopted Constitution.

The birth of Charles Thomson occurred in November 1729, in Gortede, Ireland. He was born into a devoutly Protestant family who, like many other families of the same faith, fled Ireland seeking religious freedom in America. When Charles was eleven, his widowed father, John Thomson, and his five siblings set sail for Pennsylvania. The voyage was long and turbulent and claimed the life of his father, who died after a violent struggle with seasickness. His body was tossed into the ocean just prior to reaching land, a sight that traumatized Mr. Thomson's children. Charles and his siblings were further traumatized when some of the ship's crew ransacked Mr. Thomson's luggage and stole his money, money that was to be used to establish the family in America. After their ship landed in New Castle, Delaware, the Thomson children were separated and taken in by various families in different parts of the colonies.

Charles remained in New Castle, Delaware, and over the years that followed he lived with several different families. He eventually was sent off to New London and educated in Dr. Francis Allison's academy where, in 1750, he graduated as a teacher of Latin and Greek. While at the academy, Charles came to know many men of influence, which included the likes of Benjamin Franklin. Charles espoused republican principles and the colonial cause. During the Stamp Act era, he became heavily involved with politics and rose to a leadership position within the Philadelphia chapter of the Sons of Liberty. John Adams referred to him as the "Samuel Adams of Philadelphia."

On September 1, 1774, Charles Thomson married Miss Hannah Harrison. She was the sister of Benjamin Harrison, who was one of Virginia's delegates to Congress, and one who eventually became a signer of the Declaration. A few days after their nuptials, the happy couple traveled back to Philadelphia. They had just arrived in the city when Thomson received a message from Congress requesting his immediate presence at Carpenters' Hall. Without knowing the reason for the request, he hurriedly complied, following the messenger to the assembly. Once there, he bowed before President Randolph and addressed him by saying, "I await your pleasure." Randolph replied, "Congress desires the favor of you, sir, to take their minutes." Thomson bowed in acquiescence and took his seat at the secretary's desk.

Charles Thomson was an excellent choice for secretary, serving for the better part of fifteen years. No member of Congress had a longer tenure, and through all the turmoil, he was never shaken and always displayed great confidence in the colonial cause. During his tenure he not only fulfilled the role of secretary, but he also assumed many of the roles now reserved for secretaries of state: keeping the secret journal of foreign affairs and managing the correspondence with representatives stationed abroad. Additionally, he often issued military orders on behalf of the president. In June 1782, he even designed the great seal of the United States in Congress Assembled (USCA).

When the US government was reorganized under the new federal Constitution, Charles Thomson officially retired, giving up possession of the Great Seal. This event occurred on March 3, 1788. In his retirement, he returned to his love of the Greek language and the Bible, and he translated the Septuagint from the original text into English—the Thomson Bible. The project took twenty years. In 1815, he also published *A Synopsis of the Four Evangelists, or a Regular History of the Conception, Birth, Doctrine, Miracles, Death, Resurrection, and Ascension of Jesus Christ, in the Words of the Evangelists.*

On August 16, 1824, at the ripe old age of ninety-four, Charles Thomson passed on to his reward. He was initially buried at Lower Merion, in Montgomery County, Pennsylvania, but in 1838 his nephew had his remains moved to Laurel Hill Cemetery.

THE SHOT HEARD ROUND THE WORLD

George Washington

Spring 1775

With full-scale war on the horizon and knowing that would mean a long-term commitment to Congress, George Washington put his local affairs in order. He resigned his seat in the House of Burgesses, a seat he had held for fourteen years, and equipped Mount Vernon for self-management.

In the early spring of 1775, political unrest reached a crescendo. Lines were drawn and sides were chosen. During that time, Patrick Henry delivered his famous "Give me liberty or give me death" speech at the Virginia Assembly. Meanwhile, in Massachusetts, a new provincial government had been established, a militia raised, and ammunition stockpiled. The British also were preparing for a conflict by putting a garrison of thirty-five hundred soldiers in Boston.

On May 10, Washington took his seat at Carpenters' Hall in Philadelphia, where the discussions immediately went to the recent events at Lexington and Concord—the shot heard round the world—and the Crown's "most wanted criminals," John Hancock and Samuel Adams. In the absence of Randolph and with the presidential seat unoccupied, Benjamin Harrison, from Virginia, stood up and said, "They would shew mother Britain how little they cared for her, by choosing a Massachusetts man for their president, who had been recently excluded from a pardon by public proclamation."[5] After a unanimous vote in the affirmative and Hancock's modest hesitation, Harrison took the new president by his arm, escorted him to the presidential chair, and sat him down. John Hancock became the president of the Second Continental Congress on May 24, 1775.

John Hancock

John Hancock was born in 1737 near Quincy, Massachusetts. His family was a godly family, as both his father and grandfather were ministers of the Gospel. When John was quite young, his father died and left him in the care of his paternal uncle, a wealthy businessman who lived in Boston. His uncle loved him dearly and raised him as his own son, giving him a Harvard education and subsequently employing him as a clerk within his company's accounting room. So impressive were John's abilities that in 1760, at age twenty-three, he was sent overseas on business for his uncle. During his stay in England, he witnessed both the funeral of King George II and the coronation of King George III. He attended debates in Parliament, became acquainted with leading citizens and their political sentiments, and in general, became familiar with the British hierarchical views.

In 1764, with the death of his uncle, the young businessman was called back to America. Through the inheritance left to him, he became one of the wealthiest men in Massachusetts. At that time, he began to close out his business affairs so that he might pursue politics. Elected to the Boston General Assembly in 1766, he came to know such revolutionary icons as Samuel Adams and James Otis, men who greatly influenced him. In fact, he became the primary financier of the Sons of Liberty.

It became obvious to the Crown that a man of John Hancock's means, knowledge, and influence could be a great threat to its authority in the colonies. In an attempt to sway Hancock to the Crown, the governor offered him a commission as lieutenant in the militia. Seeing the bribe for what it was, Hancock tore up the commission while in the presence of many prominent citizens, endearing him to the colonial faithful. In 1767, he was elected speaker of the assembly and then elevated to the Executive Council. However, the governor vetoed both of the appointments. In 1774, the people of Massachusetts finally got their way when Hancock was unanimously elected president of the newly established provincial government. On April 15, 1775, with the war looming over America, he called Massachusetts to a day of prayer and fasting:

> In circumstances dark as these, it becomes us as men and Christians to reflect that whilst every prudent measure should be taken to ward off the impending judgements . . . all confidence must be withheld from the means we use and reposed only on that God who rules in the armies of heaven and without whose blessing the best human councils are but foolishness and all created power vanity.
>
> It is the happiness of his church that when the powers of earth and hell combine against it . . . then the throne of grace is of the easiest access and its appeal thither is graciously invited by that Father of mercies who has assured it that when His children ask for bread He will not give them a stone.
>
> That it be, and hereby is, recommended to the good people of this colony . . . as a day of public humiliation, fasting and prayer . . . to confess the sins . . . to implore the forgiveness of all our transgressions . . . And especially that the union of the American colonies in defence of their rights, for which, hitherto, we desire to thank Almighty God, may be preserved and confirmed . . . And that America may soon behold a gracious interposition of Heaven.[6]

While Hancock was imploring divine help, General Gage, the commander of the Royal Army, was plotting his demise. Gage planned to arrest Hancock, along with Samuel Adams, who were both at Lexington, the seat of the colony's new government. Gage also planned to seize control of the rebels' munitions warehouse in Concord. When Joseph Warren, the patriot spy chief in Boston, discovered the plot, he dispatched Paul Revere, sending him on his famous ride to Lexington to warn the resistance. After Revere had delivered a warning to Hancock and Adams, he went on to alert the residents in Concord.

Hancock immediately ordered the town bell to be rung, which summoned the town's defense troops. At dawn on April 19, about 150 townsmen gathered to defend Lexington. As the skies began to lighten, eighteen hundred redcoats appeared, marching toward them. The minutemen[t] were ordered to disarm themselves, but before they could act, an unprovoked shot from the British was fired—the shot heard round the world—followed by a hail of gunfire and a return volley from the patriots. Fifteen minutes later, when the smoke cleared, ten minutemen lay dead, and many more wounded.

When the shooting began, John Hancock, who was still indoors discussing strategy with Adams, grabbed his gun and sword and started out the door. Adams pulled him back inside and convinced him that it was not their business, for they belonged to the Congress and had an obligation to get there. Convinced, Hancock fled out the back door with Adams and escaped into the woods.

The scene was very different in Concord, where 130 minutemen lay in wait for a British onslaught. They surprised the redcoats, killing 273, while losing only 49 of their own. The British panicked and fled, even though they outnumbered the patriots fourteen to one and were better trained. The Royal Army had been humiliated and had gained new respect for American soldiers.

At that time, in the middle of all the chaos, Hancock got married. With his political leadership, wealth, and handsome appearance, he had been one of the most eligible bachelors in the colonies. It was those attributes that won him an equally renowned wife, the exquisite Dorothy Quincy, daughter of the Honorable Judge Edmund Quincy. She was a bright and cultured socialite who proved to be invaluable to her husband's career.

---

[t] Minutemen: a quasi militia, consisting of town residents who could be ready to defend their community at a minute's notice.

Shortly after the Second Continental Congress had convened, Hancock became president by unanimous vote. On July 4, 1776, another unanimous vote was taken in Congress: to declare themselves as free and independent states. The Declaration was then signed by John Hancock, as president of Congress, in bold, giant strokes and sent throughout the colonies and the world. The reason for his bold signature was so, in his own words, "the British ministry can read my name without spectacles." Then he added, "Let them double their reward." He held the presidency until October 30, 1777, at which time he returned home and was commissioned major general of the Massachusetts militia. He personally saw action in 1778 with General Sullivan near Bristol Ferry in northern Rhode Island. In 1780, Hancock once again served Massachusetts when he was elected governor. He held that post until 1785, when Congress called on him to serve a second term as its president.

In 1787, Hancock returned to Massachusetts and resumed his familiar position of governor. His leadership skills were greatly needed, as the first order of business was the ratification of the Constitution. He held his office and his popularity until his death on October 8, 1793. For his extraordinary leadership and sacrifice, his countrymen will forever drape a mantle of love and appreciation over his life. It was said of his benevolence that at one time during the Revolution, he was personally supporting the families of over a hundred military men, whom Congress could not afford to pay. He outlived both of his children: a daughter who died at infancy and a son who died at age nine. Mrs. Hancock survived him by many years.

Battle of Bunker Hill

Following on the heels of the Lexington episode, another report reached the ear of Congress. The news was concerning a small group of patriots who had captured a British fort. Ethan Allen and his band of eighty-three Green Mountain Boys initiated a surprise attack on Fort Ticonderoga, a strategically located stronghold in upper New York. That small company of maverick revolutionaries believed that a successful attack on a remote fort would result in the British reinforcing all their frontier outposts, thus weakening their main army. Late one night, Allen marched into the fort, walked up to the door of the commander's residence, and awoke him with a loud knock. When the commander answered, the brave young patriot demanded that he surrender the fort. "By whose authority?" asked the commander. Allen pointed his finger to the heavens and declared, "In the name of the great Jehovah and the Continental Congress."[7] With that, the British custodian complied with Allen's command.

George Washington and his fellow compatriots of the Second Continental Congress were beginning to realize what many colonists already knew—that diplomacy, compromise, and good-faith negotiations were meaningless to a motherland bent on making an example of some of her offspring. Any doubts that still existed, regarding whether or not Congress should prepare for war, were dispelled when they received news of the Battle of Bunker Hill and the fall of General Joseph Warren.

Joseph Warren

On June 11, 1741, in the small town of Roxbury, Massachusetts, Joseph Warren was born. The Warren family was well established financially and was considered politically connected. His parents gave close attention to Joseph's education, and when his preparatory studies were completed, they placed him in Harvard, where he graduated at eighteen. He went on to study medicine and quickly earned an excellent reputation as a physician.

In 1765, when the Stamp Act was passed, Joseph's patriotic heritage caused him to side with the Whigs. Being very active and outspoken,[u] he soon established himself as one of the unofficial leaders in Massachusetts politics. In 1774, in protest of the Intolerable Acts, Boston and its neighboring towns passed the Suffolk Resolves, written by Warren and eventually endorsed by the Continental Congress. The resolves declared the Intolerable Acts to be unconstitutional and therefore void, raising the people's indignation with Parliament. The resolves also spoke against acts of violence, riots, and other licentious behavior. They further declared that the people of Boston would submit only to the authority of Congress, one of the earliest steps toward a centralized American government.

Joseph Warren was an active member of the Massachusetts Committee of Safety. As spy chief, he dispatched Paul Revere and William Dawes

---

[u] Joseph Warren was one of the earliest members of the Sons of Liberty.

on their famous ride to Lexington and Concord. When John Hancock resigned his position as leader of the Massachusetts provincial government to assume the presidency of the Continental Congress, Joseph Warren filled the vacancy.

One of Warren's first responsibilities was to build up the militia and position it for defensive purposes on the hills[v] surrounding Boston, a location overlooking the British Army. With their recent success in Concord, patriots poured into the militia from all over the colony. On June 14, 1775, Warren was appointed major general of those forces. Finding his patriot army in the forlorn state of not having more than a few rounds of shot per soldier, General Warren had to adopt a nontraditional form of defense. He immediately ordered the troops to begin felling trees and building fortifications that were low to the ground. The strategy was to have sharpshooters (men used to hunting small game with rifles) lie behind the barricades for protection and not shoot until they were sure they could hit their target. It was at that time that General Putnam gave the troops his famous Battle of Bunker Hill order not to fire until you see the whites of their eyes.

On June 17, after receiving intelligence of the American activities and feeling vulnerable, General Gage ordered a frontal attack on the patriots' fortifications. After two attempts failed with massive redcoat casualties, the British took the hill. The colonial troops retreated on the third attack, mostly due to their lack of ammunition, but not before killing 1,054 redcoats. The Americans lost only 139 men, one of whom was the beloved major general Joseph Warren.

Covered with laurels, Joseph Warren fought to his end and valiantly chose to die in combat rather than surrender to the enemy and be subjected to interrogations, indignities, and imprisonment. At the young age of thirty-four, he was the first victim of rank to fall in that great contest and will be listed at the head of those heroes who sacrificed their lives for independence. Congress, filled with sorrow over the loss of their esteemed compatriot and pitying his young family, ordered a monument to be erected in his honor and resolved to pay for the education of his eldest son. An eighteenth-century historian described Joseph Warren as follows:

---

[v] Bunker Hill was the name of one of those hills.

To the purest patriotism and most undaunted bravery; he added the virtues of domestic life, the eloquence of an accomplished orator, and the wisdom of an able statesman. Nothing but a regard for the liberty of his country induced him to oppose the measures of government. He aimed not at a separation from, but a coalition with the Mother Country. He took an active part in defence of his country, not that he might be applauded and rewarded for a patriotic spirit, but because he was, in the best sense of the word, a real patriot.[8]

The Battle of Bunker Hill produced many substantial consequences. The British were weakened and demoralized by the brave and formidable resistance of the colonials, so much so that no other major clashes were attempted for the remainder of the year. However, many acts of bullying were perpetrated by the redcoats, which included plundering and the burning of some local towns. For the Americans, and especially Congress, Bunker Hill brought encouragement. It also brought confidence to the colonial fighting forces.

THE COMMANDER IN CHIEF

George Washington

Summer 1775

The anxiously awaited reply from Congress's petition to the king had finally arrived, and the colonists' hope for an amiable solution was dashed. The king's furor was about to be demonstrated. Parliament planned to strengthen its military and naval presence in America and, once and for all, quash the rebellion. Congress had to make a decision. Was it going to surrender to a tyrannical bully who had trespassed upon its own charter or stand firm upon principle against supposedly insurmountable odds? Drawing upon the integrity and valor of the colonial citizenry, Congress chose the latter. Along with that decision came the need for an army, but who would lead it?

Up until that time, George Washington—the national icon of the French and Indian War—had chaired every military committee in Congress and was the obvious choice. Years earlier, he would have jumped at the opportunity, but at that time he was forty-four and happily settled into civilian life. On June 15, 1775, while not at all confident that he still possessed the stamina that the rigors of war would demand, he accepted the new post. With modesty and humility, he addressed Congress:

Mr. President,
Though I am truly sensible of the high honor done me in this appointment, yet, I feel great distress from a consciousness, that my abilities and military experience may not be equal to the extensive and important trust: however as the Congress desire it, I will enter upon the momentous duty, and exert every power I possess in their service, and for support of the glorious cause. I beg they will accept my most cordial thanks for this distinguished testimony of their approbation.

But, lest some unlucky event should happen unfavourable to my reputation, I beg it may be remembered by every gentleman in the room, that I this day declare with the utmost sincerity, I do not think myself equal to the command I am honoured with.

As to pay, Sir, I beg leave to assure the Congress, that as no pecuniary consideration could have tempted me to accept this arduous employment, at the expense of my domestic ease and happiness, I do not wish to make any profit from it. I will keep an exact account of my expenses. Those I doubt not they will discharge, and that is all I desire.[9]

Shortly after his appointment, General George Washington set out for Cambridge, the headquarters of the colonial forces. About one hundred miles from his destination, he was met by a delegation from the Massachusetts Assembly, who escorted him to his army. After being received with much fanfare, he gathered his troops before him for an address. His declaration, in the form of a manifesto previously prepared by Congress, set out the reasons for taking up arms against the Crown. The manifesto enumerated their grievances and then further added,

In our own native land, in defence of the freedom that is our birth-right, and which we ever enjoyed until the late violation of it; for the protection of our property, acquired solely by the honest industry of our forefathers and ourselves; against violence actually offered, we have taken up arms. We shall lay them down when hostilities shall cease on the part of the aggressors, and all danger of their being renewed shall be removed, and not before.[10]

At that point in its struggles with Great Britain, America desired restoration, not independence. Washington's commission was to defend against the hostilities of the aggressor, and by doing so, force the mother country to the bargaining table so that the previously enjoyed colonial rights might be restored. To ensure that Britain understood those motivations, Washington erected a new flag on a hill near Boston in plain view of the Royal Army. The flag contained thirteen stripes and a British Union Jack located in the upper left-hand corner. The stripes signified the thirteen united colonies, while the Union Jack signified allegiance to the Crown.

On July 2, with a desire to have God's blessing on his troops, General Washington issued his first official order to the Continental Army forbidding "profane swearing, cursing and drunkenness." In like manner, "he require[d] and expect[ed] of all officers and soldiers, not engaged in actual duty, a punctual attendance of Divine services, to implore the blessing of Heaven upon the means used for our safety and defense."[11] The colonial forces were under the command of the right man and upon a firm and moral foundation, and America knew it. Governor Trumbull of Connecticut, the only Royal governor who sided with the patriots, summed up the feelings of the colonies in a welcome letter to the new general:

> Now therefore, be strong and very courageous . . . May the God of the armies of Israel shower down the blessings of his Devine Providence on you; give you wisdom and fortitude; cover your head in the day of battle and danger; add success; [and] convince your enemies of their mistaken measures.[12]

General Washington's next objective was to prepare America for its defense, a task that had two major components. First, he needed to solidify the alliance of all the American colonies, which included the province of Georgia and the predominantly French-populated province of Canada. Second, he needed to transform his ragtag defenders of liberty into a skilled and well-disciplined army. His obstacles were numerous.

With Canada's primary population centers being occupied by the British forces, its citizens were in a position similar to that of the Massachusetts people; they felt they could not freely choose sides. The French Americans, like most of their Southern counterparts, were motivated to revolt. They were being taxed heavily and were suffering under religious persecution.[w] Although they differed in one way, they were still recuperating from the losses they had sustained at the hands of Great Britain during the French and Indian War. They just did not have the stomach for another protracted conflict, especially against the English. Congress believed, through some correspondence with prominent Canadians, that if the redcoats were

---

w   Canada's dominant faith at that time was Catholicism.

driven out of Montreal and Quebec, the French Americans would join their cause and thus create a unified American resistance. General Richard Montgomery, a highly competent former British officer, was chosen to head up the Canadian campaign.

Richard Montgomery

Richard Montgomery was born in 1736 at his family's estate near the town of Raphoe, Ireland. Few facts surrounding his childhood have survived other than as a youngster, he was afforded all the benefits customarily enjoyed by the son of an Irish gentleman, including a classical education. Upon his graduation, at only eighteen years of age, he received a commission in the British Army. The French and Indian War had erupted, so he immediately sailed for America. During his first expedition against Louisburg, he displayed such competence and heroism that he was at once elevated to the rank of lieutenant. The young officer also distinguished himself through the English victories at Montreal and Quebec.[x] In 1763, following the Treaty of Versailles,[y] Montgomery returned to England,

---

[x] During the British victory at Quebec, on the Plains of Abraham, Montgomery's leader, General Wolfe, was killed.

[y] The Treaty of Versailles, 1763 (not to be confused with a treaty of the same name that ended World War I—Germany against the Allied Powers) closed out the French and Indian War and was signed by Great Britain, France, and Spain. The French lost Canada, the Mississippi Valley, and the eastern side of the Ohio Valley to Great Britain, and they lost the western part of the Louisiana Territory to Spain (who had allied with Great Britain). Napoleon regained the territory of Louisiana for France in 1800.

where he enjoyed the appreciation and respect of his fellow citizens—rightly so, for he was a well-decorated and seasoned veteran of war.

In 1772, Montgomery sold his commission in the English Army and immigrated to America, the beautiful land he had once fought for and come to love. The tall, handsome, and highly esteemed military hero of days gone by settled in the New York area and soon after married the eldest daughter of the eminent Robert Livingston, a superior court judge. He then relocated to Rhinebeck, in Dutchess County, established a plantation on the bank of the Hudson, and devoted his full attention to his squirish duties.

The newlyweds' domestic bliss was short-lived due to the ominous clouds of political unrest that were rolling over America. In early 1775, when the gathering tempest peaked and every man was forced to choose his allegiance, Montgomery sided with his adopted country. He strapped on his sword and pistol, threw his rifle over his shoulder, mounted his steed and galloped off, leaving his teary-eyed bride to manage their many affairs. After the members of Congress chose Washington to be their commander in chief, Montgomery was called to be one of his eight brigadier generals. His sentiments at that time were preserved in a letter to a friend:

> The Congress having done me the honor of electing me brigadier-general in their service, is an event which must put an end for a while, perhaps for ever, to the quiet scheme of life I had prescribed for myself; for though entirely unexpected and undesired by me, the will of an oppressed people, compelled to choose between liberty and slavery, must be obeyed.[13]

After the capture of Ticonderoga and Crown Point, and the resulting vulnerability of Canada, Congress determined that the time was right for an offensive strike on the British forces stationed at Montreal and Quebec. General Schuyler was given command and Montgomery was chosen as his second. However, when ill health prevented Schuyler from leaving with the troops, the leadership passed to Montgomery. With a company of one thousand men, he moved in succession against the British forts at Chambly, St. John's, and Montreal, all of which fell into his hands by November 12, 1775. Through those victories, he had captured prisoners, seized vast quantities of munitions, and gained control of a large portion of Canada. Congress rewarded his brilliance by promoting him to major general.

Simultaneous to Montgomery's expedition, another company of one thousand Continentals, under the leadership of Benedict Arnold, was marching for Quebec. That expedition was quite different from that of their counterpart. There were no glorious victories for them, only one setback after another. They were shipwrecked, were chased by the enemy, were forced to wade through miles of swamp, dwindled in numbers by defections, were harassed by inclement weather, and finally starved to the point of eating their dogs. Upon arrival at Quebec, Arnold had only six hundred men remaining. He was outnumbered two to one, and worse, the British forces were fortified within the city walls. Realizing that any chance for success would hinge on his getting help, he immediately dispatched an urgent request to Montgomery for support.

Montgomery, upon hearing of Arnold's desperate situation and knowing the importance of securing Quebec, made preparations to join his comrade. Amid the blowing snows of the Canadian winter, Montgomery assembled three hundred hardy men who knew well the dangers of such an expedition. He gathered extra food and clothes—moccasins, caps, and coats—which had been captured during his latest victories. Montgomery could have remained in Montreal to hold down the fort while sending a subordinate officer to connect with Arnold, but he demanded no hardships of his men that he himself was not willing to endure. Such was his character. He put himself at the front of his troops and by example and encouragement kept his unseasoned recruits resolute in their cause. In so doing, he earned the admiration of every soldier. As he and his men trudged through the thick snow on their way to the walls of Quebec, he must have known the hopelessness of the expedition. An eerie silence was all around him, which almost seemed to be a premonition of his doom. The rendezvous with Arnold occurred on December 2, 1775.

The combined troops totaled nearly one thousand and included leaders such as Majors Livingston and Brown, and the renowned Daniel Morgan. The siege began and continued for weeks on end, but the small-caliber mortars of the Continentals seemed to have little effect on the massive walls of the fort. Disheartening as that was, things became even worse when smallpox broke out in the camp, followed by a partial mutiny. The situation was bleak. Montgomery quelled the rebellion in his usual soft, eloquent way and then called for a council of war. After all options were considered, including abandoning the expedition, both men and officers alike decided that they should attempt one final all-out assault.

A pre-dawn attack was planned for the last day of December. The strategy called for dividing the troops into four columns, two small and two large. Montgomery and Arnold had command of the two main forces, while the small groups were given to Livingston and Brown. Morgan and his sharpshooters were to assist Arnold. Livingston and Brown would strike first from the upper town and serve as a feint for the main companies, which would then attack a hopefully undefended lower town from the opposite side. When the guns from Livingston and Brown began blasting, the disciplined British forces stationed at the lower end stayed at their post rather than rushing to the aid of the besieged troops located on the upper end. By staying put, they effectively eliminated any surprise advantage the Continentals were hoping for. Minutes after Arnold began his advance, he was dropped by a musket ball that shattered his thigh. Morgan took command and fought fiercely at the head of his ranks. He was undaunted in his advance, even though he took shots through his beard and hat. His troops followed his example and gained valuable ground, inching ever closer to the walls, which they soon hoped to scale.

Meanwhile, Montgomery and his division worked their way up the banks of the Saint Lawrence River through waist-high snowdrifts to reach an area of the fortress that they had hoped would not be defended. After removing some ice barricades from their attack path, they were to charge, but instead the unseasoned soldiers hesitated. Montgomery, recognizing their timidity, shouted forth, "Men of New York, you will not fear to follow where your General leads . . . Forward!"[14] With his sword pointing toward the heavens, he rushed out in front. His astonished and devoted men followed immediately. The British responded with a flurry of grapeshot from their cannons, and when the smoke dissipated, the unmistakable, lifeless form of their intrepid chieftain, Richard Montgomery, was lying on the battlefield. His death was eerily similar to the death of General Wolf, the beloved commander of his youth, who had perished among his men sixteen years earlier, during a siege of the same city. Those who had not fallen with Montgomery turned and fled.

The British, seeing the retreat, quickly transferred their full support to their countrymen on the opposite side of the fort, putting Morgan in a dreadful situation. Even though he was overwhelmingly outnumbered, he gallantly fought on. Finally, when continuing to fight meant certain death for his men, Morgan retreated, only to find more redcoats behind him. He surrendered. The final object of the expedition had failed, leaving Canada firmly in the grasp of the British.

The people of Great Britain and America alike mourned the death of General Montgomery, for his brand of chivalry was indeed rare. An early historian described him:

> Not a stain sullied his character, and his heart was true to every sentiment of virtue, and the very seat of honor. He was but thirty-nine years of age when he fell on this disastrous field. Had he lived, he would have stood first among our military leaders, and first as a true patriot and statesman.[15]

His body was reverently buried within the walls of Quebec. It remained there for forty years until 1818, when at the request of his widow, it was exhumed and conveyed to New York. Montgomery's final resting place is in St. Paul's Church, beneath a congressionally ordered monument.

RECRUITING A COLONIAL ARMY

George Washington

January 1776

After a thorough investigation of his military, General Washington found many deficiencies. Clothes and other basic provisions were in scant supply. Military supplies such as gunpowder and bayonets were completely inadequate, and the supply of shot measured less than nine rounds per soldier. Regarding his undermanned army, Washington's report to Congress stated that "the men were able bodied, active, zealous in the cause, and of unquestionable courage."[16] However, they were comprised mostly of laymen, not used to being under authority and therefore undisciplined. They had volunteered on the condition that they could take furloughs at any time, leaving the military brass in the unenviable position of having to check with the troops before making military plans. What was worse, the entire army was enlisted only through the end of December 1775.

Congress responded with a resolution of full support for their new commander in chief and the appropriation of the needed funds. America swung into action. Supplies were sent in from every quarter, powder mills were erected and operated by women and children, and nonessential lead objects—including a statue of the king—were melted down for shot. The pulpits of almost every church in the union were ablaze with recruiting sermons—after all, it was a righteous cause. Reverend Peter Muhlenberg delivered one such recruiting sermon to his Virginia congregation on January 21, 1776.

Peter Muhlenberg

Muhlenberg was among the most prominent names in early American religious circles, as well as in Pennsylvania politics. Reverend Henry Muhlenberg, the father of Peter Muhlenberg, was one of the founders of the American branch of the Lutheran Church. In 1742, after an urgent request from the Lutherans in Pennsylvania, he immigrated to America, where he became overseer of all Lutheran churches in the northern colonies. Peter Muhlenberg, his first child, was born on October 1, 1746 in the small village of Trapp, which is located in Montgomery County, Pennsylvania. Peter was tutored to follow in his father's footsteps. At seventeen years of age, young Peter sailed for Germany, where he remained for three years, completing his theological studies. In 1766 he returned to America where, two years later, he was ordained as a Lutheran minister. A year after that, he was sent to western New Jersey to commence his pastoral duties.

Once he had established himself in his new role in the Lutheran Church, Peter decided it was time to settle down, get married, and start a family. Those dreams became reality in 1770 when he married Miss Barbara "Hannah" Meyer, the daughter of a successful potter. Together, their family was eventually expanded to include six children.

In 1771, Muhlenberg was promoted by the church and asked to take charge of a congregation at Woodstock, Virginia. However, before he could begin, he would need to be ordained by a church bishop. To facilitate that requirement, Muhlenberg immediately sailed for England, not returning until the following year. Shortly after he began his ministry at his Woodstock parish, Reverend Muhlenberg developed an interest in politics and became a member in the House of Burgesses. Many of his political views were shaped and inflamed there under the influence of his close friends, Thomas Jefferson and James Monroe. His views found their way to his constituents through his pulpit.

On January 21, 1776, at the height of a national military recruiting campaign, Muhlenberg served his country from his pulpit. He began his sermon by explaining how Great Britain had violated the colonists' inalienable or God-given rights and that it was the responsibility of Christians to do whatever they could to restore those lost rights. He then opened his Bible, turned to Ecclesiastics, and began to read from chapter 3, verse 1:

> To everything there is a season, and a time to every purpose under the heavens: A time to be born, and a time to die; a time to plant, and a time to pluck up that which is planted; A time to kill, and a time to heal; a time to break down, and a time to build up; A time to weep, and a time to laugh; a time to mourn, and a time to dance; A time to cast away stones, and a time to gather stones together; a time to embrace, and a time to refrain from embracing; A time to get, and a time to lose; a time to keep, and a time to cast away; A time to rend, and a time to sew, a time to keep silent, and a time to speak.

Then he emphatically read verse 8: "A time to love, and a time to hate; a time of war, and a time of peace." Muhlenberg then closed his sermon by quoting, "In the language of the Holy Writ, there is a time for all things. There is a time to preach and a time to fight. And now is the time to fight."[17] After concluding the service with a prayer, he removed his pastoral robe and revealed to the entire congregation that he had been wearing the uniform of a colonial soldier underneath. A drumroll was summoned, and as Muhlenberg marched to the rear of the church, he called for recruits.

When he reached the back of the church, he turned to see who had joined him. Three hundred men had stepped out of the pews and obeyed his call. Those recruits eventually became the 8th Virginia Brigade.

Muhlenberg joined General Washington in Boston, where he was appointed colonel over his newly recruited men. A year later, he was promoted to brigadier general and fought in the Battle of Brandywine. During the remainder of the Revolutionary War, he participated in many of the major battles, including Germantown and Monmouth. In July 1779, he and General Anthony Wayne stormed—and captured—the British fort at Stony Point. During the next two years, he was primarily involved with the defense of Virginia. That duty culminated with the Battle of Yorktown and the capture of General Charles Cornwallis. Muhlenberg finished the war with the rank of major general.

In 1789, after the adoption of the new federal Constitution, Muhlenberg rekindled his political aspirations and took a seat in the United States House of Representatives. As a congressman, he worked diligently and was substantially involved in the framing of the Bill of Rights. His reputation as a statesman paid dividends when, in 1801, his constituents promoted him to the United States Senate. Two years later, at age fifty-seven, Muhlenberg became the Collector of the Port of Philadelphia, a position he held until his death in 1807. His remains lie buried at a Pennsylvania cemetery near the church where he was baptized. Peter Muhlenberg's tombstone reads, "He was Brave in the field, Faithful in the Cabinet, Honorable in all his Transactions, a Sincere Friend and an Honest Man." Eighty years after his death, his statue was placed in Statuary Hall in the Capitol Building in Washington, DC.

COMMON SENSE

The year of 1775 ended with the British Army cooped up in Boston and Quebec, feeling demoralized after the series of disasters that had followed them throughout the year. They had fled from Concord, had lost numerous forts (and with them, control of large portions of the colonies), and had suffered severe casualties at Bunker Hill. The Royal government in the various colonies had been terminated and several colonial governments had been established. As demoralizing as those circumstances had been to the British, they were equally encouraging to the American ranks.

In January 1776, a new pamphlet titled *Common Sense* flooded the colonies and added more fuel to America's already flaming torch of patriotism. The publication, authored by Thomas Paine, built a strong, articulate, and compelling case for America's political independence. It provoked thousands of citizens, who had been previously uncommitted, to rethink their neutrality in favor of freedom. Within a month of the pamphlet's release, almost every provincial legislature had spoken in favor of independence. It also had become a potent instrument for the Continental Army, which had enjoyed increased enlistments because of it. Upon reading *Common Sense* and after receiving several letters from friends in Virginia, Washington wrote to Joseph Reed, saying,

[I find that *Common Sense* is working] a powerful change there in the minds of many men.[18] The sound doctrine and unanswerable reasoning contained in the pamphlet . . . will not leave numbers at a loss to decide upon the propriety of a separation.[19]

Thomas Paine

T he man, Thomas Paine, whose pen was almost as powerful as
Washington's sword during the early part of the Revolution, was born
in Norfolk, England in 1737. His father was a humble man and a Quaker
by faith. The family was of little means, and therefore Thomas's formal
education was meager at best. However, young Thomas was determined
to learn and did so through attending lectures and reading every book he
could get his hands on. He did not have access to a wide range of books, but
studied intensively on those that he had. After reading one such book about
Virginia, he stated, "My inclination from that day of seeing the western
side of the Atlantic never left me."[20] As Thomas matured, he was brought
into the family business of stay-making,[z] but that held little interest for the
young man. After leaving the family business, he found employment as
an excise officer, but did not find success in that profession. Thomas was
dismissed twice.

Thomas was not only unlucky with his early career choices, but he
seemed to be cursed in his pursuits of domestic fulfillment. At age twenty-
three, he married Miss Mary Lambert. The newlyweds were happy and

---

[z] Stays: used in the rigging of a ship, a large strong rope employed to support a
mast (*American Dictionary of the English Language* by Noah Webster, 1828).

content. However, less than a year later, Thomas's life was shattered when both Mary and their baby died in childbirth. In 1771, wedding bells rang again for Thomas when Elizabeth Ollive came into his life. Almost from the outset of their nuptials, their lives together were filled with strife, disagreements, and turmoil. Three years later, they dissolved their marriage with a formal separation agreement.

Throughout all the unfortunate events described above, Paine kept focused on his deep-seated interest in writing and debating, from which he attracted much attention. He also kept alive his childhood dream "of seeing the western side of the Atlantic." Shortly after his separation from Elizabeth, Thomas Paine's life had a dramatic turn of fortune when he made the acquaintance of Benjamin Franklin, America's diplomat to London. Franklin, like Paine, had a devout Christian upbringing and was self-educated, unsatisfied with the status quo, a free thinker, a philosopher, and an author. Paine saw Franklin as a complete man and aspired to his likeness. Franklin immediately recognized Paine's talents and convinced him that America was ripe for his pen. In 1774, with letters of introduction from Franklin, he sailed for the western side of the Atlantic. The public career of Thomas Paine was launched.

Thomas Paine established himself in Pennsylvania, Franklin's adopted province, and immediately began writing a series of articles for the local newspaper under the signature of *Common Sense*. In January 1776, at the urging of Dr. Benjamin Rush, he authored his momentous pamphlet, bearing the same expressive title[aa] as his column. His work plucked a common chord in the hearts of true patriots, who for the first time were publicly faced with a compelling and logical argument for separation from the mother country and for the establishment of a republic. The inspiring publication gave credence to those the Loyalists had labeled as rebels. Overnight, tens of thousands of copies were spread throughout the colonies. They were handed out everywhere—from the pulpits, at kitchen tables, over the fence, in restaurants, and in public squares (virtually everywhere that people had the opportunity to speak with each other). Thomas Paine had become a household name.

[aa] *Common Sense*: The pamphlet's title was at the suggestion of Benjamin Rush, signer of the Declaration of Independence and surgeon general of the Continental Army.

At the end of 1776, when the Continental Army was in a critical state and Washington was considering crossing the Delaware River for an offensive strike on Trenton, Paine's talents were once again called upon. On the eve of the attack, Washington, in an attempt to motivate his troops, ordered his men to form in ranks, after which he had the premier issue of Paine's most recent work read to them. The piece was titled *The American Crisis* and began with the words "These are the times that try men's souls." The exercise proved successful, galvanizing the troops and giving them the courage and determination to attempt the planned strike—a strike that appeared to be against insurmountable odds. *The American Crisis* eventually became a series of articles, released at critical intervals during the war.

Through his moving publications, Paine also had become a favorite of Congress, and in the spring of 1777 he was appointed secretary to the Committee on Foreign Affairs. The post was one of great trust, which in 1779 he violated by an act of indiscretion. He inadvertently leaked sensitive information that France thought might be prejudicial to their good relations with the people of America. Paine, realizing the magnitude of his mistake, resigned and returned to private life.

In 1781, Paine's powers of persuasion were called upon once again when he was asked by Congress to join Franklin on a fund-raising tour in France. The dynamic duo were at the top of their game, and vast quantities of supplies were secured and shipped to America, goods that Washington used to launch his attack on General Cornwallis during the Battle of Yorktown.

After the war, Paine continued to be employed with his pen until 1790, when he returned to his native land to visit his aged parents. Once there, he was drawn into the human rights issues that surrounded those tense political times, then prevalent in England and France. He wrote *Rights of Man*, a pamphlet that attacked the aristocratic social class, arguing that God had not created nobles and lords—men had. After two hundred thousand copies of the publication were distributed throughout England and aroused the citizenry, the Crown indicted him for treason. However, before any trial could take place, Paine fled to France, where he had become quite a folk hero. He was beginning to see himself as a citizen of the world, a freelance crusader for human injustices everywhere.

Paine arrived in France on the eve of the French Revolution and openly participated in the struggles. Unlike the American Revolution, which had a righteous foundation and was orchestrated with discipline, the French Revolution was inspired by hate and vindictive passions and directed by public hysteria. Consequently, the French Revolution spiraled out of control and was laced with continuous and random acts of brutality. The guillotine was in constant use. Paine, who could not tolerate such atrocities, even when they were perpetrated against unjust royalty, began to oppose the extreme acts of the revolutionaries. Soon, he incurred the wrath of the Jacobins[ab] and was arrested, sentenced in their kangaroo[ac] court, and finally imprisoned. He narrowly escaped decapitation.

Paine was locked up in the darkest recesses of the French dungeons with nothing to do but contemplate his predicament. His godless captors no doubt taunted him constantly, driving him to a feeling of utter hopelessness. The only way out was the way most of his fellow inmates found their freedom—through death. While he was in that distressed state of severe mental anguish, he completed his infamous work, *The Age of Reason* (a piece that he had been working on for several years). Unlike his previous writings, *The Age of Reason* lacked any sound logic or honest argument. It was a tirade against orthodox Christianity. In his perception, the Bible was often distorted to promote certain less-than-honorable agendas. The book may have been acceptable—and even appreciated—in the new secular society of France, but the people of England and America harshly denounced it. Due to his writings and his apparent conversion to the Jacobin secular philosophy, Paine was soon after released from prison and immediately began to reassemble his shattered reputation. He eventually regained his seat in the French Convention, where he served for a number of years before returning to the country of his past glory.

In 1802, Paine arrived in America and found anything but a hero's welcome. There was no fanfare when he stepped onto the New York shore. He was shunned by those he helped to liberate and ostracized by his onetime compatriots. Eight years after his notorious work, the Christian

---

[ab] Jacobins: the name that was applied to the radical political party that ruled during the French Revolution.

[ac] Kangaroo court is a mock court system whereby trials are conducted by individuals who have taken the law into their own hands, producing hasty verdicts that are unfair, are biased, and have unusually harsh punishments.

people of America were still incensed with him, as his *Age of Reason* had become a strong utensil for the enemy of their souls. It was being used as the chief publication—almost the basis—for the Deist societies that were attempting to establish themselves in America. In New York, on June 8, 1809, after years of being an outcast, Paine's turbulent life ended. Thirty years later, a monument was placed over his unoccupied grave[ad] with the following inscription: "Thomas Paine, Author of Common Sense." In summing up Paine's life, an early historian said, "As a patriot of truest stamp, his memory ought to be revered—as an enemy to that religion on which man's dearest hopes are centered, he is to be pitied and condemned."[21]

[ad] Thomas Paine's bones had been exhumed and conveyed to London.

A BLOODLESS VICTORY

George Washington
January – March 1776

In January 1776, Washington received word of the cannonade and burning of Norfolk and Falmouth, orchestrated by the Royal forces and resulting in the displacement of innocent civilians. Worse than that, Colonel Johnson, commander of the Canadian Royal Forces, had called a conference of Indian chiefs in Montreal, at which time he issued them war belts and tomahawks, inviting them and their tribes "to drink the blood, and feast on the body of a Bostonian."[22] The Indians took pride in collecting the scalps of their victims, which included women and children. Intelligence was also gathered that indicated Parliament had employed German (Hessian) mercenaries, known for their barbarity, to fight in America. It had become painfully apparent to Washington that the king was deadly serious when he said that he was planning to "utterly crush the colonial rebellion." It was with that knowledge that General Washington first spoke out publicly in favor of independence: "If nothing . . . could satisfy a tyrant and his diabolical ministry, we are determined to shake off all connections with a state so unjust and unnatural."[23] He became resolved to win the contest.

General Washington decided to drive the British from Boston and in so doing, secure another victory for his troops—a moral boost that might offset the news about the arrival of the Hessian mercenaries. By mid-February, he had his fighting force whipped into shape. They were seventeen thousand strong and enlisted for the remainder of the year. However, munitions were still in short supply.

The first step in Washington's strategy to secure another victory was to occupy Dorchester Heights, a bluff overlooking Boston and its harbor. That position would allow him to cannonade the enemy's fortifications and their battleships that were anchored in the harbor, hopefully forcing the British to retreat offshore. His plan was militarily sound, but the Continentals were missing one key component—they did not possess any cannons. Washington, however, knew just where he could acquire the missing component. A British fort at Ticonderoga was in colonial possession—Ethan Allen and his band of Green Mountain Boys had captured it several months prior. The fort would have been equipped with ample artillery pieces that could be dismantled and relocated to Dorchester Heights, but two huge obstacles would need to be overcome. Fort Ticonderoga was over one hundred and fifty miles away, and it was the dead of winter. Washington dispatched his commander of artillery, Henry Knox, to accomplish the nearly impossible mission.

Henry Knox

Henry Knox, the man history has coined the "Friend of Washington," was born in Boston on July 25, 1750. As a youngster, Henry was educated in the city's finest schools. However, that schooling was cut short at age nine due to the death of his father. From that point on, his education was limited to that which he could gain through self-study, as he was called upon to help financially support his mother and younger brother. He found work as an apprentice in a bookstore, which conveniently allowed him access to books of all subjects. His favorite subjects were history, military tactics, and the French language. He loved the bookselling industry and in 1771, he opened his own bookstore, which thrived under his strict management style.

On June 16, 1774, Henry Knox married Lucy Flucker, whose father was the Royal secretary of Massachusetts. Their joyous domestic life, which eventually included thirteen children, did not last long. In 1775, after the episodes at Concord and Lexington, Knox closed his business and fled Boston with the intent of joining the provincial militia. Knowing her husband's intentions and desiring to help, Lucy risked her life to smuggle his sword out of town. She sewed his sword into the lining of her coat and passed the Royal Guard without detection. Once he had found safety for his wife, the young bookseller-turned-patriot-soldier said good-bye and went off to serve his country.

At age twenty-five, Knox drew his sword at the Battle of Bunker Hill, where he proved himself to be a composed, disciplined, and fearless soldier. After General Washington had taken command of the Continental forces, he discovered that young Knox possessed a great deal of knowledge about artillery, most of which Knox had acquired through his insatiable interest in military books. During the autumn of 1775, Knox was promoted to commander of artillery, a position that answered directly to Washington. His first major task was to traverse one hundred and fifty frozen miles to Fort Ticonderoga (located in the extreme north of New York), dismantle about sixty of its largest cannons, load them on forty-two ox-driven sleds along with all the ammunition, and then return to Cambridge, where all his countrymen were depending on his success.

On his return trip, he and his exhausted crew fought fierce winds, snow-covered hills and valleys, and at least one disaster. While crossing one of the frozen lakes, his heaviest cannon, weighing over a ton, broke through the ice and sank. Undaunted, Knox found a way to retrieve it and then continued on his journey. The expedition took a total of forty days. Henry Knox had become one of Washington's favorite officers.

On the evening of March 4—the eve of the sixth anniversary of the Boston Massacre—Washington dispatched nearly three hundred men to the top of Dorchester Heights to set the footings for the newly acquired heavy artillery. The crew had to work in plain view of the British, but once again the hand of Providence moved, and a thick fog rolled in, hiding the men from view. The base of Dorchester could not be seen, yet above the fog the sky was clear, allowing the men to work by the light of the moon. A breeze also came up, which carried the sound of the pounding mallets away from the Royal Guard. By three in the morning, the crew finished their work and returned to the camp, at which time three hundred fresh soldiers, under Knox's command, moved the cannons up and into place. At sunrise, the Royal troops were mortified when they saw a battery of huge cannons all aimed down at them. Britain's General Howe stated that "the rebels had done more in one night than my whole army would have done in months."[24] Recognizing their vulnerability, the British quickly boarded their ships and evacuated Boston. In their haste, they left behind vast amounts of military stores. General Washington had secured his first major victory, driving the despised redcoats from Boston, and all without spilling a drop of blood.

Throughout the remainder of the war, Brigadier General Knox never left his artillery or the side of his beloved commander. His guns wreaked havoc upon the enemies of liberty at Trenton, Princeton, Brandywine, Germantown, Monmouth, and finally Yorktown. As a reward for his efforts, he was promoted to major general and selected as one of the commissioners to negotiate the terms of peace. Once peace was established, Congress promoted him to Secretary of War, an appointment he filled for eleven years. While serving in President Washington's first cabinet, he laid the foundation for the United States Navy by commissioning six warships, one of which was *Old Ironsides*.[ae] United States West Point Military Academy based its training on his ideas. He wrote the rules for civilian military training that were eventually adopted with the establishment of the National Guard.

At age forty-five, Knox retired from civil service and moved to Thomaston, Maine, where he built a home and resumed his entrepreneurial enterprises that included shipbuilding, ranching, road and river lock construction, and investing. And he still found time to dabble in state politics as an elected official. At fifty-six years of age, Knox suddenly developed an internal inflammation, and in a very short time, he fell from perfect health to sickness and then to death. Henry Knox died on October 25, 1806. A historian of his era wrote this tribute:

> [H]e was a strong man, and an officer of rare abilities; and as the friend of Washington, one who never left his side through all that gloomy period—stood by him firmly in every trial—was sworn soul and body to the common cause—he fastens himself in our affections forever. No vacillation of purpose is seen in him—no low ambitions or selfish schemes. Loving two things, his country and Washington, he ever rises before us the cool warrior, the devoted patriot, and the noble man. Washington loved him, and they never separated for any length of time, till the former retired to Mount Vernon after his public career was

---

[ae] *Old Ironsides* was the nickname for the US frigate *Constitution*, which sailed up and down the East Coast during the War of 1812. During that war, the *Constitution* enjoyed great success, capturing or destroying seven British ships. Witnesses reported that during the battles, the British cannon shot would harmlessly bounce off the hull of *Old Ironsides*.

over. He stands by him on the shores of the Delaware—moves with him over every battlefield, and finally weeps on his neck in the farewell scene in Francis' tavern. Of brilliant imagination, of strong, yet tender feelings—benevolent, brave, frank, generous and sincere; he was an honor to the enemy, to the country, and to man. As he stood a strong and high-souled youth, on the summit of Bunker Hill, so he stood amid all corruptions of a camp, and the factions of selfish men.

He was a man of much religious feeling . . . He died as he lived, an incorruptible patriot, and needs no brighter immortality than to be called

THE FRIEND OF WASHINGTON.[25]

RESOLUTION FOR INDEPENDENCE

George Washington

March – June 1776

Once Massachusetts had been emancipated from the grip of tyranny, General Washington marched his troops into Boston amid the pageantry and cheers of the townspeople. The Massachusetts Council and the House of Representatives received him with honor: "May you still go on approved by Heaven, revered by all good men, and dreaded by those tyrants."[26] Washington's response, as usual, was concise, modest, and in a proper manner. On May 10, 1776, in town hall meetings all over the province, the people of Massachusetts declared themselves independent.

When Congress got word of the "Bloodless Victory" at Boston, they were also ecstatic and, as a gesture of thanks, promptly passed a resolution to honor General Washington with a gold medal. The humble commander responded in writing: "It will ever be my highest ambition to approve myself a faithful servant of the public . . . The only reward I wish to receive [is] the affection and esteem of my countrymen."[27]

Congress, feeling much the same as the people of Massachusetts and dreaming of what could be, then took the first official step in severing the political cord with the mother country. On June 7, 1776, Richard Henry Lee, Washington's fellow Virginian, proposed a resolution for independence, and Joseph Hewes cast the deciding vote. An early historian recorded the following related anecdote:

> On the morning of the day of [the Declaration's] adoption, the venerable bell-man ascended to the steeple, and a little boy was placed at the door of [Carpenters'] Hall to give him notice when the vote should be concluded. The old man waited long at his post, saying, "They will never do it, they will never do it."

137

Suddenly a loud shout came up from below, and there stood the blue-eyed boy, clapping his hands, and shouting, "Ring! Ring!!" Grasping the iron tongue of the [Liberty] bell, backward and forward he hurled it a hundred times, proclaiming "Liberty to the land and to the inhabitants thereof."[28]

In 1751, when the Liberty Bell was molded, Leviticus 25:10 was prophetically inscribed in capital letters near its crown:

PROCLAIM LIBERTY THROUGHOUT THE LAND
UNTO ALL THE INHABITANTS THEREOF

Richard Henry Lee

The family name of Lee was one of the most prominent names in all Virginia, distinguished for wealth, intellect, and virtue. Richard's great-grandfather immigrated to America during the latter part of the seventeenth century after securing a land grant from Oliver Cromwell. Thomas Lee, Richard's father, expanded the family landholdings to include the current site of Arlington Cemetery, just three miles from where the United States Capitol Building was eventually erected. Richard Henry Lee was born in Westmoreland, Virginia on January 20, 1732, within a month of George Washington's birth and just a few miles away from Wakefield, Washington's birthplace. Both men were destined for greatness. Lee was educated in England, where he displayed exceptional aptitude for the science of politics, eagerly studying the history of all the great nations of the world, both ancient and contemporary. As a young man, he embraced the principles of civil liberty, for which he would later pledge his life, fortune, and sacred honor.

Richard was only eighteen when he returned to Virginia, where he applied himself to literary pursuits. In the early 1750s, as the colonies were preparing themselves for the French and Indian War, he raised a small military force that he commanded. When General Braddock arrived in America, Lee presented his band of volunteers for service, but was shunned by the general. Disgusted with the haughty British attitude, he and his troops returned home.

Lee's energy shifted from military to domestic pursuits, and soon after, he married Ann Aylett of Chantilly, whose family was every bit as wealthy and prominent as Lee's. Ann was a relative to George Washington through marriage, and therefore Lee and Washington became related by law, as well as by spirit. Ann died in 1767, leaving her husband to cope with four children. Two years later, Lee married Anne Pinckard and eventually expanded his family with an additional five children.

Richard Henry Lee first held public office in 1758 when he was elected to the Virginia House of Burgesses, a seat he held consecutively for seventeen years. Early in his tenure, he made a name for himself as an orator and a champion of liberty when he publicly took a stance against slavery and eloquently proposed to "lay so heavy a duty on the importation of slaves, that it would effectively stop that disgraceful traffic."[29] When the Stamp Act was introduced, he forsook his educational and social rank as an aristocrat and spoke out against it. In a letter to an English correspondent, he prophetically predicted that Parliament's aggression would backfire and lead to American independence. With words like that, he aligned himself with the likes of the powerful Patrick Henry, whose stormy eloquence greatly contrasted with the soft and persuasive rhetoric of Lee, but when combined, they were irresistible.

During the continued encroachments of Great Britain, Lee was kept fully informed of their military movements through regular correspondence with his brother Arthur, who lived in England. With that connection, the intelligence reports coming from Virginia's Committee of Correspondence were never questioned. Through that secret channel, Lee was one of the very first patriots to understand that reconciliation would never be negotiated and that only through independence would civil liberty be attained.

In August 1774, Richard Henry Lee was appointed to represent Virginia at the First Continental Congress, to be held in Philadelphia the following month. Lee served on all the important committees and, as usual, distinguished himself as one of the leaders among the many delegates, and was reelected the following year. It was during that 1775 congress that he proposed George Washington to be the commander in chief of the Continental Army. On June 7, 1776, he made a second landmark resolution:

That these United Colonies are; and of right ought to be, free and independent States; that they are absolved from all allegiance to the British Crown; and that all political connection between them and the State of Great Britain, is, and ought to be, totally dissolved.[30]

His resolution carried tremendous impact for two reasons: he represented Virginia, the most populated and wealthiest colony, and he was considered an aristocrat who had great influence among America's elite. The speeches he delivered in support of his motion were among his most effective and earned him the nickname Cicero.[af]

On June 11, four days after his resolution and while Congress was still debating the issue, he received an urgent message to return home because his wife had taken ill. That same day, Congress established a committee to put the resolution into document form, and in Lee's absence, his young protégé, Thomas Jefferson, was asked to be chairman. Lee returned to Congress in time to sign the Declaration that was spawned by his resolution.

As the war with Great Britain progressed, Lee put his faith in the hands of Providence. On November 1, 1777, the journals of Congress record that he called for a national day of thanksgiving:

> Thursday, the 18th of December next, for solemn thanksgiving and praise, that with one heart and one voice the good people may express the grateful feelings of their hearts, and consecrate to the service of their Devine Benefactor; and that, together with their sincere acknowledgements, and offerings, they may join the penitent confession of their manifold sins, whereby they had forfeited every favor, and their humble and earnest supplication that it may please God, through the merits of Jesus Christ, mercifully to forgive and blot them out of remembrance.[31]

Lee continued to be active in Congress until 1779, at which time he entered into the defense of his state by becoming lieutenant colonel of the Westmoreland County Militia. As a military leader, Colonel Lee was also

---

[af] Marcus Tullius Cicero (Roman philosopher, politician, lawyer, and constitutionalist, 106 B.C.-43 B.C.) is best known as a great political orator.

very active. In fact, General Nathaniel Greene once wrote that the British raiding parties "could not set foot in Westmoreland without having the militia immediately upon them."[32] Once, while leading a charge, he had a horse shot out from under him. Undaunted, he got back on his feet and rallied his retreating troops. He set the military standard for his descendants, one of which was the illustrious Robert E. Lee, his great-nephew.

With the arrival of peace, he again was elected a delegate to Congress, and in 1784 he was voted president of that body. When his term ended, he left Congress and returned to Virginia. He reemerged in state politics when he participated in the debate concerning the ratification of the Constitution. He sided with Patrick Henry as an anti-Federalist in opposing the Constitution because it lacked a Bill of Rights, which he believed was necessary for America's civil liberty. When the Constitution was finally ratified and put into law, he embraced it, even though there was no Bill of Rights attached. When the first Congress under the new Constitution was established, he was elected to the Senate. He served in that capacity until 1792, using his office and great influence to ensure the creation and adoption of his long-sought-after Bill of Rights.

Feeling that his life's work was complete, he retired to Chantilly, on the banks of the Potomac River. On June 19, 1794, Richard Henry Lee, at the age of sixty-four, passed on. The citizens of Virginia, as well as people from all over America, mourned the death of this great patriot. His biographer wrote, "Mr. Lee was a sincere practical Christian, a kind and affectionate husband and parent, a generous neighbor, a constant friend, and in all relations of life, he maintained a character above reproach."[33]

Joseph Hewes

The parents of Joseph Hewes were originally from Connecticut and belonged to the Society of Friends, otherwise known as Quakers. However, shortly after they were married, they decided to relocate to Kingston, New Jersey, where they purchased land and took up farming. Joseph Hewes was born on that farm in 1730. He was a studious youngster and was rewarded for his hard work by being admitted to Princeton University. At the close of his formal education, Joseph became an apprentice merchant in Philadelphia. Within a few years, he began a mercantile business on his own account with funds his father furnished him. He conducted business with the same diligence he demonstrated with his studies, and in no time he had amassed a respectable fortune.

At the age of thirty, Joseph Hewes relocated to Edenton, North Carolina, which would become his permanent residence. He established his business there and soon earned the respect of the local people. In 1763, only a few years after his relocation, the people of his community elected him to the provincial legislature, where he faithfully served for many consecutive terms. During his tenure, he took a stance against the many oppressive acts of Parliament, believing them to be "impolitic, unjust, and cruel, as well as unconstitutional and destructive of American rights."[34]

As did Lee in Virginia, Hewes understood very early in the struggles with Great Britain that the colonies would have to take drastic steps to secure their freedom. It was that perception, his outspokenness, and his skills of persuasion that caused the people of North Carolina to call a state convention for the purpose of selecting delegates to attend the Continental Congress. In the summer of 1774, that convention met and elected him to be one of the delegates, along with Richard Caswell and William Hooper. A few months later, in September, he took his seat in Congress and was immediately appointed to the committee whose task it was to draw up a Declaration of Rights. During that session, he was also active in the establishment of a non-importation agreement that he knew full well would be devastating to his personal business, which had been built on trade with Great Britain; such was his integrity. He stated, "We want no revolution. But every American . . . is determined to die or be free."[35]

The following year, Hewes was reelected to Congress. He served as a member of the Secret Committee and Naval Committee. With his extensive knowledge of shipping, he emerged as the chairman of the Naval Committee, which effectively made him the first secretary of the Navy of the United States. He personally secured a ship[ag] and appointed a captain, John Paul Jones, who became renowned for the havoc he wreaked upon British ships. For several years, Jones sailed off the Atlantic coast from Bermuda to Nova Scotia, as well as some European waters. Thus, America has Hewes, a Quaker, to thank for its first naval hero.

When Lee's motion for independence was put to the floor of Congress, Hewes found himself in the unenviable position of having to cast the deciding vote. His fellow delegates, William Hooper and John Penn, were absent due to pressing government matters at home. Consequently, North Carolina's was the last vote cast. After twelve of the colonies had cast their votes, the resolution was deadlocked: six in favor and six opposed. Up to that point, Hewes had been somewhat dubious on the point, but after searching his conscience, he cast his vote in the affirmative. John Adams described the scene: "Mr. Hewes, who had hitherto constantly voted against it, [stood] upright and lifting both hands to Heaven . . . cried out, 'It is done! [as in John 19:30] and I will abide by it.'"[36] After independence was agreed upon

---

[ag] The ship was named Providence, but Jones also commanded the Alfred and the Ranger.

and the Declaration drawn up, he joyfully placed his signature upon that glorious parchment. Over the next few years, Hewes submerged himself in congressional work. He often labored twelve hours a day, without stopping for even a meal. He wrote, "My country is entitled to my service, and I shall not shrink from her cause, even though it should cost me my life."[37]

In the spring of 1779, Hewes suffered a terrible tragedy. He had been engaged to Isabelle Johnson, sister of Governor Johnson of North Carolina. Just a few days before they were to be wed, she suddenly died. Hewes never recovered from his broken heart. He immediately returned to Congress, where he could serve his other love, America. He resumed his hectic and grueling schedule, which eroded his already weakened constitution. In October 1779, with his health failing rapidly, he resigned his seat. Being too sickly to travel, he remained in Philadelphia, where he died eleven days later. He died on November 10, 1779, at the age of fifty. He was buried in Philadelphia in the cemetery of Christ Church, after a public funeral in which a large procession of citizens gathered with Congress to pay their final respects and to bid their patriotic friend farewell.

CHARLESTON STANDS FIRM

As Congress was debating independence, Washington and his troops, along with the colonial faithful, were filled with anxiety as they anticipated the king's unbridled wrath. Where would he strike first? With the high concentration of Loyalists in New York and South Carolina, the possession of those two colonies would be of great strategic importance to Britain. Washington eventually discovered that General William Howe's attack plans for the colonies would be prosecuted on dual fronts. He would march against the middle colonies with his main army, while at the same time he would send a smaller force to the Carolinas under the command of General Henry Clinton. Howe assumed that Clinton's forces would be augmented by enlistments from the Southern Loyalists.

In early February 1776, Clinton set sail from Boston with fifteen hundred troops, bound for Cape Fear, North Carolina. An integral part of his expedition was the idea of connecting with the Southern Loyalists. He arrived in late February only to find that the Loyalists had suffered a substantial defeat at the hands of the North Carolina militia. Realizing that the local allies were in no mood to join his forces, Clinton decided that he would move on to South Carolina. However, before proceeding south, he requested additional naval support. His reinforcements arrived in early May, at which time the combined forces sailed for Charleston.

Earlier in the spring, when Congress received word from Washington that the Royal Navy was sailing for the Carolinas, they dispatched General Charles Lee to take command of the Southern forces. About the same time, John Rutledge—having just been granted leave from Congress so that he might attend to his gubernatorial responsibilities—returned to South Carolina and began arranging for the defense of Charleston. Rutledge raised funds, stockpiled ammunition, reorganized the militia, and named some new officers. He also ordered a fort to be constructed on Sullivan's Island. The fortification would serve as the primary shield for the Charleston Harbor. When Lee finally arrived in Charleston, he found the provincial militia assembled and well organized under the competent command of Colonel William Moultrie.

William Moultrie

William Moultrie was especially motivated to protect Charleston, as it was his place of birth, an event that occurred on December 4, 1730. His parents possessed above-average wealth and strong Royal connections that helped secure the governorship of St. Augustine for William's brother. In 1749, at age nineteen, William married Elizabeth Damarius de Julien. They would eventually have three children, one of whom died in infancy.

William Moultrie was indoctrinated into public life at the early age of twenty-one, when he was elected to the South Carolina Provincial Assembly. Moultrie also served South Carolina through the military and saw his first action during the French and Indian War. At age thirty, he displayed bravery and strict discipline while fighting the Cherokee Indians and was rewarded with a promotion to captain. Simultaneously, Francis Marion—another of the South's favorite military men—was named as his lieutenant. Moultrie's experience in doing battle in the backwoods and swamps of the frontier prepared him well for his leadership role with the state militia and for the hardships he would endure later as a prisoner of war.

Moultrie, having Huguenot ancestry, possessed much empathy for the persecuted and, therefore, naturally became a Whig. He was active in civic duties and was a bold voice for republicanism right up to the beginning of the Revolution. When the hostilities with Britain became certain, the South Carolina Provincial Assembly earmarked one million dollars for the purpose of raising a militia and appointed Moultrie as colonel of the South Carolina militia. Moultrie's appointment occurred on the same day that the Battle of Bunker Hill was fought.

In the spring of 1776, Moultrie was ordered to build a fort on Sullivan's Island, a strategic site from which the defense of Charleston could be mounted, as no ship could enter the harbor without first passing by it. Thousands of spongy palmetto logs were obtained from the nearby forest on the mainland and then rafted over to the island. A crude fort was then constructed. It was approximately five hundred feet long and only sixteen feet wide. When General Lee arrived from the North, he inspected the dugout-shaped structure and described it as a "slaughter pen." He warned Moultrie that it would not hold up, saying it would be nothing more than a pile of splinters thirty minutes after the commencement of the Royal Navy shelling. However, Lee's negativity could not convince Moultrie to abandon his fort. The undaunted colonel was outfitted with 31 cannons and 435 men. Lee positioned himself a safe distance away, with the idea of managing the inevitable retreat.

On the bright and sunny morning of June 28, nine Royal ships of war confidently cruised down the coastline from the direction of Cape Fear. The Royal vessels were equipped with 256 guns—the smallest gun was equal to Moultrie's largest. The fleet paused broadside to the low-rise fort—not knowing what to make of it—when all at once the colonial artillery blasted forth a murderous round of cannon shot upon the perplexed seafarers. A volley was returned, and the thunderous battle was on. General Lee, who was watching from a distance, was astonished when, hours later, the "slaughter pen" was still intact. More than that, Moultrie's novice artillerymen were inflicting strike after strike upon their mighty British foe.

As the lead from the more than two hundred guns pelted the fort, Moultrie's troops kept calm and fought back like veterans. They drew their confidence from their seasoned commander. Occasionally, as Moultrie sauntered back and forth in the corridor behind his cannons, shouting his orders, he would pause, pull out his pipe, and coolly puff away while surveying the situation. Nothing escaped his perpetual awareness. After his men had enjoyed a brief rest, he would put away his pipe and resume his pacing and the barking out of his commands.

The fierce and incessant cannonade continued all day and into the evening. The darkness that fell on the battle scene enhanced the spectacle. At every discharge, flames would be seen bursting out from the mouth of the cannons, followed by a scarlet arc, chasing the shot's trajectory. And when the molten lead hit its target, the resulting explosion was equally spectacular. After eleven hours and no sign of weakness from the colonials, the crippled fleet pulled up anchor and quietly retreated out to sea. When Moultrie's intrepid colonials realized the enemy had fled, they belted out a hearty cheer of victory.

The morning light revealed the remains of the whipped fleet, the abandoned and burning hull of the British battleship *Acteon*. As the battle-fatigued garrison reveled at the sight, the *Acteon* suddenly exploded, showering the area with fragments of timber. Later, Governor Rutledge and the men and women of Charleston came to the fort and heaped praise on the intrepid defenders of their fair city. One distinguished lady presented Colonel Moultrie with a pair of elegant colors, saying,

> The gallant behavior in the defense of liberty and your country, entitles you to the highest honor . . . and I make not the least doubt, under Heaven's protection, you will stand by them as long as they can wave in the air of liberty.[38]

General Lee could hardly contain his delight, even though his personal involvement amounted to nothing more than his futile plan for a retreat. South Carolina had only thirty-six militiamen killed or wounded, while the Royal Navy lost over three hundred men. After the humiliating and unequivocal defeat at Fort Moultrie, Great Britain left the South, allowing it to be free from hostilities during the first few years of the Revolution. Britain did not return to Charleston until the spring of 1780, when it began a month-long siege of the city.

In September 1776, Moultrie was promoted to the rank of brigadier general in the Continental Army. In that new capacity, he would answer to General Charles Lee. General Moultrie, although not involved in any other major conflicts, was continually in the field from that point until the siege of Charleston. When Charleston fell, he was taken prisoner and held at

St. Augustine. While there, Great Britain attempted to secure his services. Knowing he would never turn against his fellow patriots, they offered him a foreign commission in exchange for his freedom. His response reflected his patriotism:

> When I entered this contest, I did it with the most mature deliberations, and with a determined resolution to risk my life and fortune in the cause. The hardships I have gone through I look back upon with greatest pleasure. I shall continue to go on as I have begun, that my example may encourage the youth of America to stand forth in defence of their rights and liberties. You call upon me now, and tell me I have a fair opening of quitting that service with honor and reputation to myself, by going to Jamaica. Good God! Is it possible that such an idea could arise in the breast of a man of Honor? I am sorry you should imagine I have so little regard for my own reputation, as to listen to such dishonorable proposals . . . You say by quitting this country for a short time, I might avoid disagreeable conversations, and might return, at my own leisure, and take possession of my estates for myself and family. But you have forgot to tell me how I am to get rid of the feelings of an injured honest heart, and where to hide myself from myself.[39]

Such was his integrity.

General Moultrie was held prisoner for two years, until the close of the war, when he was freed through an exchange. For his patriotism and courage, Congress appointed him to the high rank of major general. When peace was declared, he retired to private life, where he enjoyed the tranquility of his home and family. However, he was pulled back to the public arena when the good people of South Carolina bestowed on him their highest honor by electing him governor in 1785—and again in 1794. William Moultrie died on September 27, 1805, in his seventy-fifth year of life. He was remembered as a stoic, resolute leader who was as brave as a man could be. His biographer heralded his life:

His integrity as a statesman and public officer was a bright example; his disinterestedness was beyond praise. His fellow citizens honored him with trust, reverence, and his intimate acquaintances loved him for his many private virtues. The infirmities of age at length admonished him to retire to private life . . . Like a bright sun setting without an obscuring cloud, the hero and sage descended peacefully to his final rest.[40]

William Moultrie was buried at Windsor Hill Plantation, his son's property. On June 28, 1978, his remains were reinterred on Sullivan's Island near the waters he so valiantly defended. The state of South Carolina has opened a visitor center at the same location.

DECLARATION OF INDEPENDENCE

George Washington

July 1776

On July 2, 1776, two days before the Declaration of Independence was unanimously accepted by Congress, General Washington, acting on his own instincts, delivered the following communiqué to his troops:

> The time is now near at hand which must probably determine whether Americans are to be freemen or slaves, whether they are to have any property they can call their own, whether their houses and farms are to be pillaged and destroyed, and they consigned to a state of wretchedness from which no human efforts will probably deliver them. The fate of unborn millions will now depend, under God, on the courage and conduct of this army. Our cruel and unrelenting enemy leaves us no choice but a brave resistance or the most abject submission. This is all we can expect. We have therefore to resolve to conquer or die. Our own country's honor [calls] upon us for a vigorous and manly exertion, and if we now shamefully fail we shall become infamous to the whole world. Let us therefore rely upon the goodness of the cause, and the aid of the Supreme Being in whose hands victory is, to animate and encourage us to great and noble actions. The eyes of all our countrymen are upon us, and we shall have their blessings and praises if, happily, we are the instrument of saving them from the tyranny meditated against them. Let us therefore animate and encourage each other and show the whole world that a freeman contending for LIBERTY on his own ground is superior to any slavish mercenary on earth.[41]

One week later, Washington announced to his troops that Congress had formalized his sentiments, as well as the mood of the country, by the Declaration of Independence. He stated that that momentous event should "serve as a fresh incentive to every officer and soldier to act with fidelity and courage, as knowing that now the peace and safety of his country depends (under God) solely on the success of our arms."[42] The final drafting of the Declaration of Independence was the handiwork of his fellow Virginian, Thomas Jefferson.

Thomas Jefferson

The grandfather of Thomas Jefferson immigrated to America from Wales in the mid-seventeenth century and settled in Chesterfield, Virginia. Thomas Jefferson was born on April 13, 1743, the firstborn of his parents, Peter and Jane Jefferson. At five years old, he entered grammar school,[ah] where he prepared himself for a traditional education. His study of the classics began when he was nine, under Reverend William Douglas, a Scots clergyman, but was cut short when his father died in 1757. At the young age of fourteen, Thomas became the head of his family and superintendent of Monticello. With the added responsibilities, he was forced to continue his education under a personal tutor, Reverend Maury. In 1763, after attending the College of William and Mary for two years and impressing his professors, he began an apprenticeship in law under the acclaimed George Wythe. Through his relationship with his mentor, he became acquainted with many leading men of Virginia and became the personal friend of the governor.

[ah] A "grammar school," also known as "Latin school," taught students the rules for writing intelligibly and that they may thoroughly understand what they are reading.

He seemed destined to be a Tory[ai] until one day in 1765, when he heard Patrick Henry's famous Stamp Act speech. From that day on, he determined in his heart to be counted among the patriots by making a stand for freedom. In 1769, he was elected to the Virginia House of Burgesses, where he served the public faithfully until the Revolution.

In 1772, he married Martha Skelton, the widowed daughter of John Wales, an eminent Virginia lawyer. Martha was three years younger than Thomas. An early biographer described her at the time as being beautiful, gracious, educated, and multitalented. Together, they would have five children to brighten their lives.

During the last few years leading up to the Revolution, Jefferson's pen was very active. He was a member of the Committee of Correspondence and in 1774 published a pamphlet titled *A Summary View of the Rights of British America*. That pamphlet was addressed to the king and was extremely offensive to all Loyalists, so much so that the governor threatened to charge him with high treason. Through his pen, he gained national notoriety and, in 1775, he was elected a delegate to the Second Continental Congress. The following year, in a peculiar chain of events, he became the primary participant in the drafting of one of our country's most historic documents, the Declaration of Independence.

A few days after Richard Henry Lee proposed independence, Congress established a committee to draft the resolution. Lee, who no doubt would have been selected as chairman, was absent due to his wife's illness. Consequently, the privilege fell to his fellow Virginian and friend, Thomas Jefferson. Jefferson, who was one of the youngest delegates, was joined on the committee with such illustrious members as Benjamin Franklin, John Adams, Roger Sherman, and Robert R. Livingston. Franklin, who was first called upon to pen the document, declined the privilege because, as he stated, "I will not author a document that will be subject to review and change." The next choice was Adams, but he felt that he had alienated too many delegates with his strong opinions, and therefore the resolution would have a better chance of being approved with a different author. Jefferson's notorious pen put him third in line, a task he accepted without hesitation.

[ai] A Tory was a friend of the Crown and therefore politically aligned with the British Parliament.

With the momentous task at hand, Jefferson locked himself in his quarters for the weekend, where he wrote, edited, amended, reedited, and finally rewrote the Declaration. The preamble was drawn from a common source—as many parts of it have been found in earlier political documents—and was widely accepted by the delegates. Once it was completed, Jefferson sent a draft copy to his old law professor, mentor, and fellow delegate, George Wythe, for his review. Jefferson relied heavily on the instruction he had received years before from Wythe, who in turn was a disciple of Montesquieu,[aj] Blackstone,[ak] and Locke,[al] all of whom were well-read European legal scholars.

The Declaration was next scrutinized by the committee (changes were made) and then presented to Congress for additional scrutiny (Congress made more changes). Although 70 percent of the sentences were changed (altered, removed, or amended) in some form, the general format and intent remained similar. The language was softened, and the references to God were quadrupled. Congress wanted its citizens and soldiers, and all of Europe, to be reminded that the Revolution was based on a righteous footing.

On July 4, 1776, Congress unanimously agreed to the Declaration, which announced to the world that the United States of America was a free and independent nation. Four days later, Jefferson wrote Lee, to whom he owed his great favor:

[aj] Charles-Louis Montesquieu (French lawyer and political philosopher, 1689–1755) believed in the separation of state powers: executive, legislative, and judicial.

[ak] Sir William Blackstone (judge, jurist, and Tory politician, 1723–1780) was a legal scholar famous for his volumes of written commentaries on British law.

[al] John Locke (British political philosopher, 1632–1704) believed in "government with the consent of the governed," which was interpreted by James Otis, Patrick Henry, and other likeminded revolutionaries to include taxation—meaning taxes could not be levied without the consent of the governed. Therefore, "taxation without representation is tyranny."

Philadelphia, July 8, 1776

To Richard Henry Lee, Esq.

Dear Sir, . . . I enclose you a copy of the Declaration of Independence, as agreed to by the House, and also as originally framed; you will judge whether it is the better or the worse for the critics . . . I shall hope to see you, . . . in convention, that the business of government, which is of everlasting concern, may receive your aid. Adieu, and believe me to be, your friend and servant,

Thomas Jefferson[43]

Later that summer, Jefferson resigned his seat in Congress and returned to Virginia, where he was elected to the General Assembly. Throughout the remainder of the Revolution, he served his state by participating in the committee whose function it was to revise the Virginia laws, establishing schools for general education, and confirming rights concerning freedom of religion. He succeeded Patrick Henry in 1779, becoming the second wartime governor of Virginia. His memorable accomplishments were few due to the unsettling environment of British occupation. In fact, during the latter part of his gubernatorial term, his cabinet was constantly harassed and pursued from one meeting place to the next by the marauding enemy.

In 1782, he was again elected a delegate to Congress where, the following year, he served as chairman of the committee that reviewed the treaty with Great Britain. Congress unanimously ratified the treaty based on the committee's report. While in Congress, he also authored an essay on coinage and currency, outlining the current denominations of money and the dollar as a unit, suggestions that were eventually adopted by the government.

His reputation grew to international stature in 1784, when he was appointed minister to the French court. He sailed for Paris, where he succeeded Benjamin Franklin and, while there, he became very popular among the literary circles and upper society. He returned in 1789 to find America buzzing over the recently adopted federal Constitution and a new president, his fellow Virginian, George Washington. Washington immediately offered Jefferson a seat in his new cabinet as secretary of state, which he cautiously accepted. He proved to be a very useful and efficient aide to the president, but he resigned in 1793, choosing not to serve for a second term.

In 1796, having developed a reputation as a staunch anti-Federalist, Jefferson ran for the presidency against John Adams, who was a Federalist. Among the many candidates, Adams secured the most votes and Jefferson the second-most votes, and thus Adams became president and Jefferson became vice president, as was the custom at that time.

In 1800, Jefferson ran again for the presidency and won. He held that office for two terms, finally retiring from public office in 1808. As with most two-term presidents, his first term was more effective. The landmark of his presidency was the purchase of the Louisiana Territory from France, accomplished largely through the diligent work of Robert R. Livingston, minister to France. He also appropriated federal funds to pay for Christian missionaries to evangelize the Indians; his thinking was that if you could convert them to Christianity, America would not need to fight them. In fact, he personally authored a tract titled *The Life and Morals of Jesus Christ of Nazareth* to be given to the Indians. During his stay in the White House, he also served as president of the Washington, DC public school system. In that capacity, he instituted the use of Bibles and *Watts Hymnals*[am] as primary reading texts. His rationale was "I have always said, and always will say, that the studious perusal of the sacred volume will make us better citizens."[44] He made it clear to everyone that the "wall of separation" between church and state was to be a one-way wall—the state should not govern the church, but the church was welcome in government.

Upon his retirement, Jefferson returned to Monticello, where he spent the remaining seventeen years of his life enjoying his family and hobbies. His hobbies included reading, writing, inventing, and botany. He accumulated a large library and always seemed to have several books by his side in various stages of being read. In fact, he invented a four-sided tabletop book stand that swiveled so that he could close one book, turn the stand and open the next book without getting out of his chair. He wrote volumes of articles, on almost every topic, as well as letters to friends and family. His botanical gardens included plants from all over America. In 1818, he also founded the University of Virginia, locating it near Monticello, and served as rector until his death.

[am] The *Watts Hymnal* was the first purely American hymnbook, which included the Psalms put to music.

During the spring of 1826, his health deteriorated to an extent that he was confined to his bed. Early in the month of July, feeling that he would not recover, he inquired as to what day of the month it was. Being told that it was the third, he expressed a great desire to live until the next day so that he might breathe the air of the fiftieth anniversary of his country's independence. His wish was granted. The next morning, he softly thanked his friends and family for their devotion and care and then declared, "I resign myself to my God, and my children to my country."[45] He never spoke another word and departed this world at around noon on July 4, 1826. Remarkably, his fellow committee member (the committee who was tasked with drafting the Declaration) John Adams died that same day, at almost the same hour.

Thomas Jefferson died at the age of eighty-three. His biographer wrote of him, "In religion he was a free thinker; in morals, pure and unspotted; in politics, patriotic, honest, ardent and benevolent."[46] His tombstone reads,

Here was buried
THOMAS JEFFERSON,
Author of the Declaration of Independence,
Of the Statute of Virginia for Religious Freedom,
And Father of the University of Virginia.

Here are two of Jefferson's most well-known quotes:

And can liberties of a nation be thought secure when we have removed their only firm basis—a conviction in the minds of the people that these liberties are the gift of God? That they are not to be violated but with His wrath? Indeed I tremble for my country when I reflect that God is just: that His justice cannot sleep forever.[47]

* * *

I am a real Christian, that is to say, a disciple of the doctrines of Jesus.[48]

PART III

The Signers of the Declaration of Independence

SIGNING THE DECLARATION OF INDEPENDENCE

During the spring of 1776, the legislatures of each colony held in-depth debates concerning the topic of independence. To most, the path forward was clear. One by one, each colony passed resolutions and wrote new instructions for their congressional delegates in Philadelphia. The instructions reflected their new feelings toward independence. In most cases, the shackles were completely removed from their delegates, and they were allowed the freedom to consult openly with the other colonies regarding independence. Most delegations were also given the authority to vote with the majority, even if the majority was in favor of independence.

After the king received intelligence concerning the changing mood of his American colonies, he decided to absolutely crush the rebellion. Parliament engaged thousands of German mercenaries and sent them, along with a large portion of the British Army, across the Atlantic for the purpose of snuffing out every vestige of colonial resistance to the Crown. The king would make an example of his obstinate American colonies, to such an extent that his other colonies around the globe would never consider a similar rebellion.

On July 4, after weeks of thorough debates, the Continental Congress unanimously voted for the Declaration of Independence. John Hancock, the president, then signed that glorious document and subsequently sent it throughout the colonies and Europe. General Washington received his copy on July 8 and immediately ordered his troops to be assembled for the news. That evening, as he sat calmly on his gray-white steed at the head of his army, the Declaration was read among the cheering Continentals. Meanwhile, back in Philadelphia, Congress ordered the Declaration to be entered into the Journals of Congress. As a show of solidarity, it was decided that the signatures of all the delegates would be added to the bottom of the parchment. The signing ceremony was scheduled for August 2.

Prior to the scheduled date of the signing ceremony, Congress received word of the British Navy's arrival off the shores of New York. The delegates assumed that Britain was just waiting for a reason to begin doling out their special vengeance upon the ringleaders of the rebellion. Undaunted, Congress moved ahead with its plans.

The congressional signing of that cherished document was a solemn act, requiring the utmost patriotism and determination, as it would be considered treason by Great Britain and punishable by death. As Charles Thomson, the secretary of Congress, called out each name—grouped by state delegation—the beckoned statesman came forward to the signing table and added his signature to the Declaration, pledging his life, his fortune, and his sacred honor in the cause of freedom. During the ceremony, Benjamin Franklin reminded Congress, "We must now all hang together, or we shall most assuredly hang separately."

Josiah Bartlett

The sparsely populated province of New Hampshire sent only two delegates to the Continental Congress: Josiah Bartlett and William Whipple, both strongly in favor of independence. On June 15, 1776, New Hampshire's legislature unanimously instructed their delegates to join with the other colonies concerning independence. When the signing ceremony took place in August, New Hampshire was the first group of delegates to be called to the signing table, and Bartlett was the first of that illustrious brotherhood of American patriots to sign the Declaration of Independence.

The Bartlett ancestral records date as far back as the eleventh century. In 1066, William the Conqueror and Adam "Bartellot" (the ancient version of Bartlett) sailed from the district of Lisieux in Normandy and fought together at the Battle of Hastings. Over the next many centuries, members of the Bartellot family are identified in periodic military records, including those of King Edward III. In 1634, John and Richard Bartlett, along with their families, immigrated to America. Richard, Josiah Bartlett's great-great-grandfather, settled in the Newbury area and took up the trade of shoemaking. His son, Richard Bartlett, Jr., was born in England and was only fourteen when he arrived in America with his father. In 1679, he was elected into the colonial legislature, marking the beginning of the Bartlett family's involvement in American politics. His son, Richard, was born in 1649. He was the third of that name and was the grandfather of our subject.

The father of our subject, Stephen Bartlett, was born on April 21, 1691. He and his wife, Hannah Webster (an early relative of the statesman Daniel Webster), lived in a large house in Amesbury Ferry, where they raised seven children. Of the seven children, Josiah was the youngest. He was born on November 21, 1729. Josiah did not receive a formal education, but was privately tutored by a relative, Reverend Dr. John Webster. Although his education was not formal, it was thorough—he even gained a good understanding of Greek and Latin. At sixteen, Josiah began the study of medicine. He launched his medical practice in Kingston, New Hampshire, in 1750. Within several years, Dr. Josiah Bartlett had the reputation of being a skillful practitioner.

In 1754, Josiah married his first cousin, Mary Bartlett. She was well educated and turned out to be a masterful administrator, managing the family home and farm while raising their twelve children (eight reached adulthood). With Mary supervising the family enterprises, Josiah found the time to shift his interests to politics. He became a member of the New Hampshire provincial legislature in 1765. With the Bartlett family having lived in America for over one hundred years, it is not surprising that he took a Whig stance and was a dependable supporter of the colonial causes. He strongly opposed the Stamp Act and consequently rose to a leadership position in the legislature.

After the Lexington and Concord violence, the New Hampshire governor dissolved the assembly and fled the state, abdicating his authority and leaving the state without any form of governance. Soon after, a new provincial congress was formed—Josiah Bartlett led this movement. In August 1775, he was sent to Philadelphia as a delegate to the Continental Congress. The following year, Bartlett voted for Lee's resolution and later signed the Declaration.

In 1777, Bartlett shifted his efforts to the military by providing medical assistance to General Stark in Vermont. After the Battle of Bennington, Bartlett returned to Congress. In November, he was privileged to have the opportunity to vote for and sign the Articles of Confederation. The following year, he asked for leave that he might attend to his personal affairs that had suffered in his absence—he never returned to that body.

A short while after arriving in his home state, Dr. Bartlett opened a new chapter in his life when he was appointed to the bench in New Hampshire. He became the chief justice of the court of common pleas. In 1782, he rose to the superior court, where he served for six years before being elevated to the seat of chief justice. When the question of ratification of the Constitution was put before the state, he took a leading role in its adoption. Once the new federal government was in place, Bartlett was elected to the Senate. However, he declined the honor due to his bench duties. In 1790, the crown of his public service was achieved when the people of New Hampshire elected him as their chief executive—two years as president, followed by two years as governor (New Hampshire changed the title for their chief executive midway through Bartlett's term).

In 1794, Bartlett retired from public office so that he might enjoy his declining years in the close proximity of his family. However, they did not enjoy his retirement long, for on May 19, 1795, the great statesman passed on to his reward. He was sixty-five years of age. His tombstone reads:

Patriot, Scholar, Statesman
A delegate to the Continental Congress
A signer of the Declaration of Independence
With Stark at Bennington
A member of the Convention which ratified
the Constitution of the United States
Chief Justice, President, and first Governor of New Hampshire
Not more illustrious for public services
than for private virtues . . .

Matthew Thornton

During the latter part of the 1776 summer, the New Hampshire Provincial Congress—having just been organized at the beginning of the year—decided to add a third member to their congressional delegation. In September, Matthew Thornton, their Speaker of the House, was appointed to be that delegate. He arrived in Philadelphia in November, five months after the Declaration of Independence had been adopted and during one of the darkest times of the Revolution. At that late date, Thornton was not obligated to sign the Declaration, and by not signing, he could have spared himself the bounty that the British placed on the head of every signer. However, Thornton so agreed with each and every word of the Declaration that, at his request, he was permitted the honor of signing[an] the birth certificate of this great nation. Thus, the New Hampshire delegates were the first and last to sign.

Matthew Thornton was born in 1714 in Ireland and immigrated with his parents to America at the age of three. They eventually settled

---

[an] Matthew Thornton's signature is not located in the upper right-hand signing area with the two other New Hampshire signers. Due to his late date of signing, his signature can be found on the bottom of the far right signature column, under Oliver Wolcott's.

in Worcester, Massachusetts, after living a few years in Wiscasset, Maine. Young Matthew's preparatory education groomed him for entering into the profession of medicine. After just a few years of establishing his practice in Londonderry, New Hampshire, he had become a very well-known physician and had amassed substantial wealth. In 1745, he became a surgeon with the New Hampshire militia, accompanying the troops on their expedition against Louisburg, Nova Scotia. Upon his return, Governor Wentworth rewarded him by appointing him colonel of the militia, as well as justice of the peace.

At the age of forty-six, Dr. Thornton married Hannah Jack, a young woman who was also of Irish descent. Over the next few years, Dr. and Mrs. Thornton had five children, four of whom reached maturity.

After the members of the New Hampshire provincial legislature sent delegates to the First Continental Congress, Governor Wentworth retaliated by dissolving that body. However, the Whigs, who were by far the majority, caused the governor to fear for his safety. In early 1775, he fled the state and in so doing abdicated his authority. The Whigs later reorganized in what they called the provincial congress, but in the interim they elected Matthew Thornton as its temporary president. When the new provincial government was in place, Thornton became speaker of the house, the highest office in that newly established body. During that same year, he was appointed judge of the provincial superior court and chosen to be a congressional delegate. He was subsequently sent to Philadelphia. He was reelected to the Continental Congress in 1777, where he remained for one additional year, after which, at the age of sixty-three, he resigned. He continued in the office of judge until 1782 before permanently resigning from public life.

At age eighty-one, he was struck by a severe case of whooping cough, which left a weakness in his lungs and caused him to be susceptible to pulmonary disease. Other than that, he enjoyed excellent health all of his life. On June 24, 1803, at the ripe old age of eighty-nine, Matthew Thornton passed away, having outlived his wife by seventeen years. They were both buried at Thorntons Ferry, New Hampshire. His contemporary biographer said this of him: "Dr. Thornton was greatly beloved by all who knew him, and to the close of his long life was a consistent and zealous Christian."[1]

Robert Treat Paine

Massachusetts was the second colony to allow their congressional representatives to vote for independence. The delegates were allowed to vote in favor of Lee's resolution if they thought it was necessary for the safety of the united American colonies. The General Assembly of Massachusetts issued those instructions to their delegates on May 10, 1776. The five signers from Massachusetts were John Hancock, John Adams, Samuel Adams, Elbridge Gerry and Robert Treat Paine—the least famous member of the Massachusetts delegation. All, except Samuel Adams, were affluent men with substantial property holdings. As the president of Congress, Hancock was the first of the Massachusetts delegation to sign the Declaration, which he did on July 4—the other four had to wait for another month.

Robert Treat Paine was born in Boston in 1731, the maternal descendant of Connecticut's Royal Governor Treat. Being the son and grandson of clergymen, Robert was given an early theological education. At fourteen, he entered Harvard, where he met and studied with John Hancock and Samuel Adams. Harvard was a fine institution for those who wanted a Christian education, which is what Robert's father desired for his son. Some of Harvard's requirements included the following:

Let every student be plainly instructed and earnestly pressed to consider well the main ends of his life and [study] to know God and Jesus which is eternal life, John 17:3, and therefore to lay Christ in the bottom as the only foundation of all sound knowledge and learning.

Everyone shall so exercise himself in reading the Scriptures twice a day that he shall be ready to give an account of his proficiency therein.[2]

At eighteen, Robert graduated with honors and shortly after worked on the sea as a merchant marine. During his time working on a ship, he was able to see the southern colonies, as well as Spain and England. Upon his return to America, he entered the teaching profession. He later shifted his career to the ministry and in 1755 joined the military as a chaplain. Not long after, he took up the study of law under the instruction of Benjamin Pratt.[ao] In 1757, he became a member of the Boston bar and later moved his practice to Taunton, where he also became involved in politics. Eight years later, he found himself in opposition to the radical measures of the Stamp Act and a strong opponent of the president of the Massachusetts Assembly. Through it all, Paine earned a reputation as being a staunch Whig.

In 1770, Robert married Sarah Cobb, a native of Taunton and the well-to-do daughter of Captain Thomas Cobb. Like her father, Sarah's brother also had a notable military career, as he served three years as an aide to General Washington. Robert and Sarah had eight children: four boys and four girls.

Robert Treat Paine's public life began in 1774, when he was elected a member of the Provincial Assembly of Massachusetts, where he was an active and enthusiastic patriot. His efforts were rewarded immediately by being chosen as a delegate to the Continental Congress. The highlight of his congressional tenure was the signing of the Declaration of Independence. He resigned from Congress at the end of 1776 and returned to Massachusetts, where he served as Speaker of the House in the state legislature.

Once Paine returned to state politics, he expanded his responsibilities to include the bench. He was soon after appointed attorney general, a post he

---

[ao] Benjamin Pratt was a notable jurist who eventually became the chief justice of New York.

held until 1790. Paine was also a member of the Massachusetts Convention, where he helped frame the state's constitution. His last public office was that of judge of the Massachusetts Supreme Court, where he sat until 1804, retiring because of deafness.

Robert Treat Paine enjoyed his retirement for ten years before he passed away in 1814. In his Last Will and Testament, he declared:

> I am constrained to express my adoration of the Supreme Being, the Author of my existence, in full belief of His Providential goodness and His forgiving mercy revealed to the world through Jesus Christ, through whom I hope for never ending happiness in a future state.[3]

The life of Robert Treat Paine will be remembered not only for his political endeavors, but also for his theological writings. The titles of his two books were *The Divinity of Christ* and *Salvation Through Christ*. As a theologian, he was proud of the Christian foundation of America.

Elbridge Gerry

With the mood of the American people having shifted toward independence, many of the state legislatures decided to replace their passive-minded delegates. The two new delegates from Massachusetts were John Hancock and the lesser-known Elbridge Gerry—both were unwavering patriots. Gerry did not arrive until February 1776, but immediately made his presence felt. He was extremely vocal—on the floor of Congress, as well as in small private meetings—and convinced many of the undecided delegates that freedom would be achieved only through independence. In fact, John Adams said, "If every man [in Congress] was a Gerry, the Liberties of America would be safe against the Gates of Earth and Hell." On August 2, during the signing ceremony, the Massachusetts contingent was the second group to be called to the signing table. The last of the Massachusetts delegation to sign was Elbridge Gerry.

Thomas Gerry, the father of our subject, immigrated to America from England in 1730 and settled in Marblehead, Massachusetts. He was a successful merchant, controlling ships and extensive trading routes. He also maintained a leadership role in both state politics and the local militia. Elbridge Gerry's mother, Elizabeth, was from the Greenleaf family who were also heavily involved in the mercantile industry. Together, Thomas and Elizabeth had eleven children, though only five reached adulthood.

Elbridge Gerry was born in Marblehead, Massachusetts, on July 17, 1744. He was given an excellent education that began with private tutors, continued with an undergraduate degree from Harvard in 1762, and culminated with a master's degree three years later. Soon after, he entered the family business, whereby he amassed a handsome fortune of his own. His business success, superior intellect, and high ethics earned him the trust of the good people of his community. Even though his business relied heavily on trade with Great Britain, he was extremely vocal about the burdensome taxation policies of Parliament. He willingly entered into non-importation and non-exportation agreements, which were created to counter the Crown's encroachments. During those years, he was in constant communication with all the leading patriots of Massachusetts and soon became completely obnoxious to the Royal government, but he was loved by the common folks.

In 1772, Gerry's public career was launched when he won a seat in the provincial general court. While in the legislature, he demonstrated great energy and a special gift for devising complex plans for the execution of all the Whig-inspired resolutions. He was always a fierce opponent of the Crown. In fact, he established Marblehead's Committee of Correspondence—the second such network in the province (after Boston). During the summer of 1774, he was chosen as a delegate to the First Continental Congress, but chose not to attend due to the recent death of his father.

The people of Massachusetts finally got their way when Gerry arrived in Congress in the early part of 1776. He supported Lee's resolution and signed the Declaration on August 2. The following year, he became more involved with the Continental Army, visiting the troops at Valley Forge and then rallying for their support before Congress. In 1783, with the War of Independence effectively won, Gerry resigned from Congress so that he might attend to his personal affairs and business, both of which had suffered in his absence.

As Gerry settled back into civilian life, his focus shifted to his domestic fulfillment. Ann Thompson, a young lady who was twenty years his junior, came into his life. She was from a wealthy New York family who was also in the mercantile business, so they had much in common. They were married in 1786 and eventually brought ten children into the world.

The Constitutional Convention that was convened in Philadelphia during the summer of 1787 attracted statesmen from every corner of the union. The people of Massachusetts once again called upon Gerry to represent their interests. In that body, he was one of the most vocal members, which was completely consistent with his nature. He argued for a distinct line between the state governments and federal authority, and he fought against the latter gaining too much power. He also was disturbed by the absence of clauses that would protect the individual rights of the people—so much so that at the conclusion of the convention, he refused to sign the Constitution. There were only a few members who took such a strong stance. He had developed a reputation for being opposed to a large central government—Gerry had become an anti-Federalist.

With the Constitution adopted, Gerry took his opposition down to the state level. He published a letter—which was widely circulated—detailing his opposition to it. However, once the Constitution became the organic law of the United States of America, he embraced it. He was immediately elected to the House of Representatives, where he toiled tirelessly for the Bill of Rights. He remained in that body until 1792, after which he semi-retired and returned to his home, where he could once again experience the domestic joys of his young family. Other than a short assignment to France (under President John Adams) as an American commissioner, he remained in Marblehead until 1810, when he was elected governor of Massachusetts. It was a narrow victory. Gerry was victorious again in his 1811 campaign, but lost his reelection bid in 1812, even though that same year his party swept the state senate—the success they enjoyed was due solely to one of Gerry's vintage "complex plans."[ap]

[ap] Elbridge Gerry's "complex plan" required some redistricting of the Massachusetts political map into odd shapes in order to secure the most possible votes for his party. On March 26, 1812, the *Boston Gazette* published a political cartoon in which the Essex County state senate district was depicted as a strangely shaped animal—one complete with wings, claws, and a dragon's head—to bring attention to some of Gerry's newly drawn districts. The wording in that cartoon included "Gerry-mander." It was the first time the word had been used, and since then, the term "Gerrymandering" has always been used in conjunction with any political party redrawing district maps for their constituent's voting advantage.

In 1812, the same year Gerry lost his governorship, he was asked to run with James Madison as his vice president. He was chosen because the party believed he could deliver the northern vote. He did, and Madison went on to win an easy reelection. Gerry was sworn into office in March 1813, but did not survive his first term. On November 23, 1814, Elbridge Gerry died from a hemorrhage of the lungs while fulfilling the responsibilities of his office. He was buried in the Congressional Cemetery, Washington, DC.

Stephen Hopkins

Stephen Hopkins can be easily identified in any depiction of the signers due to the hat he always wore, a Quaker tradition. His signature on the bottom of the Declaration of Independence also can be easily identified—it looks like a signature from a trembling hand. Hopkins's signature on the Declaration was not his normal signature. His normal signature was graceful, flowing, and very legible. In fact, Hopkins was renowned throughout the colonies for his exquisite handwriting. Was he then gripped with fear as he signed? Certainly not! At the time of signing, Hopkins was sixty-eight years old—the second oldest signer after Franklin—and had suffered a stroke, leaving him with some paralysis on his right side (he was right-handed). When his name was called to come forth and sign, he got up from his chair, shuffled up to the signing table, took the quill pen with his left hand, and signed his name into history. With his physical impairment, he had a good excuse not to sign, and no one would have questioned his patriotism. His sense of duty, however, required his presence alongside his Rhode Island colleague, William Ellery. Rhode Island's congressional delegation was the third group to sign the Declaration.

Stephen Hopkins was born near Providence, Rhode Island on March 7, 1707. Although he was the grandson of a Baptist minister, he was raised a

Quaker. The rural setting of the family farm provided limited access to any type of formal education. However, through his superior intelligence, he overcame that adversity. In his early twenties, Stephen married Sarah Scott, who was also a Quaker.

At that time, Stephen Hopkins made his livelihood on his farm, but in 1731 he relocated to Providence, where he pursued the mercantile business. Almost from the outset, his business was sidetracked by politics. He held various offices over the next thirty-five years, including being a member of the General Assembly, speaker of the General Assembly, chief justice of the court of common pleas, chief justice of the superior court, delegate to the Continental Congress, and finally governor of Rhode Island. He was also the founder of the Providence town library.

In 1757, at the height of the French and Indian War, Governor Hopkins became extremely active in the recruitment of soldiers. At fifty, he even took a captain's commission and, later that year, found himself at the head of one of his volunteer corps. By the Stamp Act era, Hopkins had taken a decided stance on the side of the colonies, alienating himself from the Royal provincial government. The stance, however, was quite submissive, as seen in his literary work *The Rights of the Colonists Examined.*

> We finally beg leave to assert that the first planters of these colonies were pious Christians; were faithful subjects; who with a fortitude and perseverance little known and less considered, settled these wild countries by God's goodness and their own amazing labors [and] thereby added a most valuable dependence to the Crown of Great Britain . . . but all have honestly obeyed every royal command and cheerfully submitted to every constitutional law . . . no kingdom or state hath, or ever had, colonies more quiet, more obedient, or more profitable, than these have ever been.[4]

The colonial faithful believed that Great Britain—not them—were guilty of violating constitutional law by attempting to raise taxes without representation.

In 1774, he further alienated himself from the Crown when he intro-duced a bill to the state legislature that would prevent the importation of slaves, a bill that was intended to eventually put an end to the practice of the slave trade.[aq] Although the bill failed to pass, Hopkins, believing in freedom and liberty for all, emancipated his slaves.

Hopkins was elected a delegate to the Continental Congress in 1775. He had tremendous insight regarding the struggle with the mother country and how it would be settled. In May 1776, knowing that words would never secure liberty, he predicted "blows must decide, or powder and ball." During that same month, the Rhode Island legislature instructed their congressional delegation to join with other colonies in pursuit of independence. Rhode Island was the fourth colony to unshackle their representatives. A few months later, Hopkins voted for and signed the Declaration of Independence. Hopkins remained a delegate until 1779 and was on the committee that prepared the Articles of Confederation. He then retired from public life at seventy-two. Stephen Hopkins died on July 19, 1785, leaving his wife, Ann,[ar] and five children from his first marriage. Biographers of his day honored him:

> He went to his grave honored as a skillful legislator, a righteous judge, an able representative, and dignified and upright Governor.[5]
>
> [As an] affectionate husband, and a tender parent, he was greatly attached to the regular habits of domestic life. Exemplary, quiet, and serene in his family, he governed his children and domestics in an easy and affectionate manner . . . As in life he had despised the follies, so in death he rose superior to the fears of an ignorant and licentious world; and he expected with patience and met with pious and philosophic intrepidity the stroke of death.[6]
>
> Through life he had been a constant attendant of the religious meetings of Friends, or Quakers, and was ever distinguished among men as a Christian.[7]

[aq] The slave industry was of utmost importance to the profitability of England's import and export industry. By pushing slave labor on the plantation owners, they could keep the cost of their imported products lower.

[ar] His first wife, Sarah, died in 1753, and Hopkins married Ann Smith in 1755.

Roger Sherman

On June 14, 1776, Connecticut called for a special assembly to decide the state's position on the question of independence. On that day, Connecticut's General Assembly unanimously passed a resolution allowing their congressional delegates to vote for independence. As such, Connecticut joined the ranks of four other states that also had passed similar resolutions.

After Lee's resolution for independence was thoroughly debated on the floor of Congress, a committee was established for the purpose of putting the resolution into written form. Congress chose some of its most illustrious and most patriotic members: Roger Sherman, Benjamin Franklin, John Adams, Robert R. Livingston, and Thomas Jefferson. With the committee's work completed, the Declaration was adopted and then signed by John Hancock. Copies of it were then sent throughout the colonies, Canada, and Europe. Each member of Congress would later sign that cherished document.

During the signing ceremony on August 2, the fourth group that came up to Charles Thomson's table was the delegation from Connecticut. The four delegates were: Roger Sherman, Samuel Huntington, William Williams, and Oliver Wolcott. Each bravely endorsed the Declaration, pledging their lives, their fortunes, and their sacred honor.

On April 19, 1721, Roger Sherman was born on the family farm that was located near Newton, Massachusetts. Two years later, Roger's parents moved to Stoughton (less than 20 miles south of Boston). Roger's early education consisted of the knowledge that he was able to glean by studying the books in his father's library, a few years of grammar school, and the private tutoring of his pastor, Reverend Samuel Dunbar.[as] During his youth, Roger accepted an apprenticeship as a shoemaker, but it was cut short in 1741 when his father died. At only nineteen, Roger was left to manage the small family farm. Three years later, the family sold the farm and relocated to New Milford, Connecticut, where his elder brother lived. Roger made the trip on foot, carrying his shoemaker's tools on his back.

Once the family was settled into their new community, Roger forged a partnership with his brother. They opened a general store—the first in New Milford. With the extra time that entrepreneurship offered, Roger doubled down on his love affair with books, reading every one that he could get his hands on. He proved to have an aptitude for learning, as he was able to retain almost all of what he read. Within a few years, Roger had become one of New Milford's leading citizens. Roger developed a special fascination with the subject of law and after a few years of self-study, he became a member of the bar in Litchfield.

With his professional life on the fast track, Roger turned his interests to romance. In 1749, he married Elizabeth Hartwell, the daughter of Joseph Hartwell, who was a deacon in the Church of Stoughton. She was known for her Christian character and was loved by all who knew her. She and Roger would have seven children before Elizabeth's untimely death in 1760. Marriage bells rang again for Roger in 1763, when he and Rebecca Prescott were wed. Rebecca was twenty years his junior and eventually gave him eight more children. She turned out to be the perfect helpmate for Roger, as she was able to manage their household affairs effectively, allowing him to concentrate on all his civic responsibilities.

During the twenty years that followed Roger Sherman's relocation to New Milford, he became one of Connecticut's leading citizens, holding many important positions, including member of the state's General

---

[as] Samuel Dunbar (1723 Harvard graduate, ordained pastor of the Church at Stoughton, served as a chaplain during the French and Indian war, 1704-1783) was a true patriot and supported the colonial cause throughout the Revolution.

Assembly, justice of the peace, judge of the county court for Litchfield, treasurer of Yale College, and finally state senator. He served as senator during the turbulent Stamp Act era and fearlessly sided with the Whigs.

In 1774, a new chapter began in Sherman's political career when he was elected to represent Connecticut at the First Continental Congress. When he arrived at Carpenters' Hall on September 5, the first order of business was to formalize the gathering. Congress accomplished this through a document they titled the Articles of Association—or simply the Association. The document created a system whereby the represented colonies could act in unison. The document also imposed trade boycotts against Great Britain, which were designed to force Parliament to the bargaining table so that the colonies might get the Intolerable Acts repealed. The Association's goal was to gain relief from Britain's burdensome policies without severing their allegiance to the Crown. Sherman—along with all the other members of the First Continental Congress—placed his signature on the Articles of Association, which took effect on December 1 of that year.

The king and Parliament reacted negatively to Congress, choosing to retaliate by sending its military to America to deal with their insubordinate colonies—the act that spawned America's independence. During the summer of 1776, Sherman voted for and signed the Declaration. Sixteen months later, he also affixed his signature to the Articles of Confederation. He continued to be an active member of Congress until peace was achieved, at which time he returned to Connecticut and resumed his bench duties. Soon after, he also undertook the colossal task of revising the Connecticut laws so that they may comply with the new state constitution.

In 1787, with the country slipping into economic and political chaos, statesmen from all over the union gathered in Philadelphia to participate in the Constitutional Convention, where they hoped to correct the country's negative trajectory. Sherman was among the numerous attendees. At sixty-six, he filled the role of a senior statesman (Benjamin Franklin was the only attendee who was older). Sherman was terse and infrequently animated in his comments, but that did not hamper the stabilizing effect his presence had on the proceedings. At the conclusion of the convention, Roger Sherman endorsed America's new operating bylaws. His signature on that document carried much weight throughout the United States.

After the Constitution was ratified, Sherman served his country in the House of Representatives for a period of two years, after which he was elevated to the Senate. During his tenure in Congress, the Bill of Rights was created and attached to the Constitution. Roger Sherman died in his sleep on July 23, 1793. His passing occurred after a two-month period of illness—his death was reportedly due to typhoid fever, however, his physician suspected that his death was due to a "disorder . . . seated in his liver." He was seventy-two years of age.

Roger Sherman holds a unique distinction among the Founding Fathers. He was the only person to affix his signature to each of the four great founding documents: the Articles of Association, the Declaration of Independence, the Articles of Confederation, and the federal Constitution— and being a member of the First US Congress, he also played an integral part in the establishment of the Bill of Rights.

William Williams

Signing the Declaration of Independence was a serious exercise, a treasonous act that was considered a capital offense for which the penalty was death—by way of hanging. The conversation below helps to demonstrate the serious reality of the signers' pledges. It occurred a few months after the signing during a Council of Safety meeting—it was one of the darkest hours of the Revolution.

> "If we fail," said Mr. Williams, "I know what my fate will be. I have done much to prosecute the war; and one thing I have done which the British will never pardon—I have signed the Declaration of Independence; I shall be hanged." "Well," said Mr. Huntington [another member of the Safety Council—not Samuel Huntington], "if we fail I shall be exempt from the gallows, for my name is not attached to the Declaration, nor have I ever written anything against the British Government." "Then sir," said Colonel Williams turning upon him, "you deserve to be hanged for not doing your duty."[8]

The great-great-grandfather of this patriot immigrated to America in 1637 and settled in Roxbury, Massachusetts. William Williams was born on April 18, 1731. Both his father and grandfather were Congregational ministers, so it is not surprising that William enjoyed a godly upbringing. At sixteen, he entered Harvard College, from which he graduated with honorable distinction four years later. He then began the study of theology, but before he could finish, his attention shifted to the French and Indian War, which had just erupted.

The war plucked a patriotic chord within William's soul, and he felt obligated to do his duty and serve his country. He subsequently joined the militia. After enlisting, he found himself under the leadership of his relative, Colonel Ephraim Williams. During the war, he witnessed many of his countrymen die, including the colonel, which burned the realities of battle into his young mind. Through that experience, William made two other observations. First, it was obvious to him that the Royal forces felt they were superior to their American counterparts. Second, he noticed a lack of sympathy by the British for the brave colonial patriots who sacrificed their lives. William finished his commission with the rank of colonel.

When William returned to civilian life, he took up the mercantile business in Lebanon, Connecticut, where he earned quite a name for himself in the community. That fine reputation helped launch his public career. At twenty-five, he became town clerk, a position he held for most of his life. Public service seemed to agree with him because, in 1757, he was also elected to the statehouse, an office he held for nineteen years.

In 1771, William Williams married Mary Trumbull, the daughter of Governor Jonathan Trumbull.[at] Mary was a beautiful young debutante who was well educated and was a great help to him in all his political endeavors. Governor Trumbull's home became known as the War Office of the Revolution, with visitors such as Samuel Adams and George Washington coming and going regularly. With company like that, it was inevitable that Williams would become heavily involved in the struggle for independence.

In 1775, Williams was chosen to attend the Continental Congress, where he joined the other Connecticut delegates. Knowing the seriousness of the times and the high stakes involved, he closed out all his business affairs so

---

[at] Jonathan Trumbull was the only Royal governor to support the colonies in their struggle for independence.

that he might devote himself completely to the cause. The following year, he voted for and signed the Declaration of Independence. During the years of the Revolution, Congress asked him to sit on the Committee of Safety, a post for which he was well suited, considering his military background. Near the end of the war, he converted his large house into a barracks for the soldiers, while he and his wife relocated to a small residence—an arrangement that continued until the end of the war.

When the war was over and America had won its independence, it needed a new form of government. Williams again stepped forward and in 1788 took a leading role in Connecticut's ratification process for the new Constitution. He voted for the adoption of the Constitution even though his constituents were opposed. However, before long, they realized the wisdom of his position, at which time they applauded him for his foresight and statesmanship.

For sixteen more years, Williams was active in Connecticut politics, finally retiring from public service in 1804. He declined reelection and returned to private life, where his wife, three grown children, and many grandchildren enjoyed his constant companionship. After only a few years of domestic tranquility, his life was shattered by a major tragedy when his eldest son, Solomon, died suddenly. Williams became greatly demoralized and died less than a year later. William Williams's death occurred on August 2, 1811, with his last words being the name of his son, which he repeated over and over until he passed away.

William Floyd

The four delegates from New York who signed the Declaration of Independence were William Floyd, Philip Livingston, Francis Lewis, and Lewis Morris, all of whom were considered aristocrats. However, even though they were all part of upper society, as compared to their counterparts from New England, they possessed the Dutch Reform work ethic of their forefathers. They were all involved in the mercantile business, and all owned large landholdings where they lived in elegant, estate-type homes. Assemblymen in New York at that time were paid only about six shillings per day, hardly enough to interest men of their means. Their motivations came from a sense of duty and patriotism. At the time of the signing, those delegates were well aware that the British armada was sitting just off the shores of New York, ready to retaliate against any rebels who might sign the Declaration. For them, their pledge of life and fortune was very real. Floyd said he knew that he was devoting his "fine farm and mansion and valuable timber to the special vengeance of the British commanders,"[9] but self-interest played no part in his motives.

Great were the personal sacrifices of William Floyd. His vast landholdings were the first to feel the brunt of the British retaliation. His mansion was used as an enemy meeting place, his crops and livestock were completely depleted by the hungry British troops, and his beautiful grounds were totally trampled. His wife and children were forced to flee and live in exile for seven years, a situation that proved to be fatal for his wife, who at only forty-one years of age died from extreme physical hardship and anxiety.

Wales was the homeland of this patriot's ancestry, who immigrated to New York late in the seventeenth century. His grandfather, who was a wealthy agriculturalist, settled in Setauket, on Long Island. He acquired a large tract of land for the purpose of farming. That tract of land became the family seat, and it was there, on December 17, 1734, William Floyd was born. His affluent family afforded him an excellent education, but before he could enter a profession or business of his own, his father died and left him to manage the extensive family estate. His integrity and management skills were noticed by all, and soon after he was called to public office. Floyd's opposition to British tyranny endeared him to the populace.

In 1760, William Floyd married Hannah Jones, who not only bore him three children, but also displayed a great capacity for administration, in that she managed all her husband's personal affairs, allowing him to concentrate on the public's business. They both enjoyed entertaining at their estate house, which incidentally had a very close proximity to Francis Lewis's property. With that location, their connections, and their hospitality, their house soon became the central meeting place for many of the local gentry. As a prominent member of society, he graciously accepted his leadership role. Floyd was slow and methodical, as well as logical and practical in his political philosophies, which once established were unwavering.

Floyd's sentiments and political philosophies fell opposite of the Crown and, consequently, he was a natural choice when New York chose its delegates for the Continental Congress. When Congress's reconciliation attempts failed and war became imminent, he was given the command of the Suffolk County militia and served on the front lines until he was promoted to the rank of general. He left his command in 1776 to give full attention to his congressional duties. In Congress, he was very active on many committees and eventually voted for and signed the Declaration of Independence.

In 1777, General Floyd gave up his seat in Congress and returned to state politics. Months later, his integrity, sound judgment, and exceptional financial management skills landed him on a committee whose task it would be to rescue the state of New York from its near-bankruptcy condition.

He and the rest of his committee were able to steer the state around its economic problems that were caused by the Revolution. In 1780, Floyd returned to Congress, where he served for three additional years.

Once tranquility had been reestablished in New York, Floyd returned to his estate, but found it in such a devastated condition that he chose not to restore it. Instead, he purchased a tract of land on the Mohawk River, where he built a new house. He remarried[au] and had two more children. Over the next thirty-seven years, Floyd remained somewhat active in politics, including a few terms as state senator, an office he held until the year before his death, which occurred on August 4, 1821. William Floyd died at the age of eighty-seven, enjoying excellent health and a sharp mind until his end.

[au] William Floyd's second wife was Joanna Strong—she was thirteen years his junior and eventually gave him two more children. Hannah Jones, Floyd's first wife, died in 1781 from exposure, fatigue, stress, and illness—the hardships she experienced while living in exile.

Francis Hopkinson

U nlike the New York delegates, who were primarily upper class, the New Jersey delegates were a very diverse group. They were drawn from the upper and middle class and as such were a much better representation of the country. After Washington's success in Boston, the general attitude of the colonies shifted from reconciliation to independence, and New Jersey was no exception. The people of New Jersey decided to replace their congressional representatives with new delegates who were more receptive to the changed mood. John Hart was reaffirmed, while John Witherspoon, Richard Stockton, Abraham Clark, and Francis Hopkinson were all newly selected. When the vote for independence was taken in Congress, the New Jersey delegation was unanimously in favor.

Francis Hopkinson was a man who possessed a wide scope of talents. He was an attorney, judge, public official, writer, poet, artist, and musician. In his chosen profession of law, he eventually rose to the position of United States federal judge. As a public official, he earned the confidence of the people of New Jersey and was chosen to represent them at the Continental Congress, where he toiled for independence. He authored many writings, most of which displayed great wit and humor, which endeared him to the populace. Many of his writings were political in nature. In fact, John Adams credited Hopkinson's pen with "irresistible influence" in the struggle for freedom. Utilizing his musical talents, he was chosen as the music director and choir leader at the church he attended. He was also responsible for the first purely American hymnal, dated 1767, in which he put each of the 150 Psalms to music.

Francis Hopkinson was born into a godly home, the Christian foundation of which was established by his grandfather, who was the bishop of Worcester. His ancestors were included in England's high society, and when his parents immigrated to America, they continued their familiar social status. His father, an intimate friend of Benjamin Franklin, was the judge of the Vice Admiralty Court. His mother was a relative of Lord North, the member of the British Parliament who authored the infamous Tea Act. Hopkinson was born in Philadelphia on September 3, 1737, and was raised in a way consistent with a young aristocrat. He was only fourteen when his father died, which caused him to mature quickly. In 1757, after graduating with honors from the University of Philadelphia,[av] he chose law as a profession and within four years was admitted to the bar. He was soon practicing law before the Supreme Court of Pennsylvania. His legal reputation and writings caught the attention of Britain, and consequently, he was chosen as a member of the Governor's Council, a lucrative government post in New Jersey. He soon after moved his residence to that state.

With his law practice and political career flourishing, he turned his attention to romance and the pursuit of domestic fulfillment. His success in this venture is described in the following excerpt from the *Pennsylvania Chronicle and Universal Advertiser*:

Bordentown, Sept. 3

On Thursday last Francis Hopkinson, Esq., of Philadelphia, was Joined in the Velvet Bonds of Hymen, to Miss Nancy Borden, of this place, a lady [known] both for her internal as well as her external accomplishments and in the Words of a celebrated Poet: "Without all shining, and within all white, Pure to the sense, and pleasing to the sight."[10]

[av] Francis Hopkinson's father helped establish the University of Philadelphia.

Nancy Borden and her sister were said to be the most beautiful women in New Jersey. She and Francis settled down and eventually expanded their family to include five boys and four girls. The Borden family was also politically well connected. Nancy's father was the Honorable Judge Borden, an active patriot and a member of the 1774 Revolutionary Convention. Her sister, Maria, married Thomas McKean, a signer of the Declaration of Independence. With Hopkinson's many talents, coupled with the Borden influence, it was no wonder that he became a leader in America's struggle for freedom.

As his republican principles grew in both word and deed, Hopkinson quickly became an irritant to Great Britain and was removed from his position in the Royal government, an act that further endeared him to the hearts of the people. In 1776, he was elected a delegate to the Continental Congress where he voted for and signed the Declaration of Independence. Later that same year, he was appointed chief justice of New Jersey. Those actions and his new colonial appointments brought on British retaliation. His home was ransacked and then used as winter quarters for the British officers, thus sparing it from total destruction.

In 1779, Hopkinson returned to Philadelphia to assume his duties as judge of the Court of Admiralty, a position he held for ten years. A decade later, when ratification of the Constitution was placed before the people of New Jersey, he zealously supported it with tongue and pen. In 1790, under the newly organized judiciary, President Washington appointed him judge of the United States District Court for Pennsylvania. He did not serve long in that capacity, for on May 9, 1791, his illustrious life was terminated. Francis Hopkinson died after a severe attack of apoplexy—he was only fifty-three. His wife and five of his children survived him. Nancy lived until 1827. His biographer described him as follows:

> Mr. Hopkinson was one of the most modest, quiet men, on whom the mantle of true genius so infrequently falls. Although ardent in his patriotism and keenly alive to the events in the midst of which he was placed, yet he seldom engaged in debate; and his public life is not marked by those varied and striking features, so prominently displayed in the lives of his compatriots.[11]

John Hart

As Speaker of the House of the Continental Congress, shortly after the signing of the Declaration, John Hart stated, "We look for the permanency and stability of our new government to Him who bringeth princes to nothing and teacheth senators wisdom."[12] Honest John, as he was generally known, was one of the nine signers who never witnessed the fulfillment of independence. Hart, a Baptist deacon, filled the role of a spiritual leader among his compatriots. Once, when the revolutionaries were almost overcome with worries—they had no navy and no army, and they were about to take on the most powerful force in the world—John prayed and rebuilt their confidence. In his prayer, he called on God to be their ally and then reminded Him that they were doing the right thing and that their motives were righteous. He ended his prayer by prophetically stating that God would bring them victory.

Edward Hart, the father of John, was a patriot in his own right. He was the leader of the volunteer corps known as the Jersey Blues, who in 1759 helped General Wolfe defeat the French at Quebec, winning Canada for England. John Hart was born in Connecticut in 1711, but that was his home for only a short while, because a year later, his parents relocated to Hunterdon County, New Jersey. Not much is known about the childhood of John, except that he grew up on a farm, which he later inherited, and that he had very little formal education. In 1740, John married Deborah Scudder, who bore him thirteen children. By 1760, John was farming about four hundred acres of prime land and operating two gristmills. He was well-known for his benevolence and was the primary supporter of his church, donating the land upon which it was built. Compared to some of the signers, he was not considered rich, however, he was the wealthiest and most respected man in his farming community.

John Hart first appeared on the public stage in 1761, when he became judge of the New Jersey Court of Common Claims, an office he held for fifteen years. During the same time, he also occupied a seat in the Provincial Assembly. When the Stamp Act frenzy swept through the colonies, John sided with the Whigs, stating that he would feel like a slave if he were taxed even *to the value of a straw* without representation. In 1774, at the age of sixty-three, he was chosen to attend the First Continental Congress, where he became Speaker of the House and a strong advocate for independence. Just prior to Congress's vote for independence, New Jersey replaced their delegates—except for Hart, who was reaffirmed—with representatives who were more republican minded. Shortly after, he voted for and signed the Declaration of Independence. In early October of that year, he received an urgent message that his wife had become very sick and that she was requesting his return home. He left Philadelphia immediately and arrived home in time to find his wife alive, but deathly sick. Deborah passed away on October 8.

In November 1776, while the British troops were chasing Washington through New Jersey, they decided to dole out some of their special vengeance upon one of the ringleaders of the rebellion. John Hart lived in that part of New Jersey. In an attempt to preserve the life of their aged patriot, Hart's neighbors coaxed him to flee the area. Although Hart was still mourning the death of his wife, he reluctantly accepted their advice and became a fugitive. Hart fled just in time to escape the enemy. Employing the use of tracking dogs, they pursued him for days, but when they were unable to find him, they returned and pillaged his farm. Hart evaded the British for months, never staying in the same place more than one night, for fear of the danger it would bring upon those who would harbor him. He spent many nights in caves or under the stars, with only leaves for cover. Due to their unsuccessful efforts to capture him, the frustrated British authorities offered Hart a pardon in exchange for his surrender. That pardon, however, was contingent on his recanting of the Declaration. John Hart's integrity would not allow him to even consider it.

After the Battle of Trenton, the British left the area. Assuming the threat had passed, Hart returned home to find his house and barns burned, his farm ravaged, and his livestock plundered. Worst of all, his children and their families had been scattered by war and captivity. John Hart did not complain about his great losses or his personal sacrifices, for he had kept his pledge to his county: his life, his fortune, and his sacred honor. So great was the adversity he faced that he gave up his will to live, and a short time later, he died. After John Hart's death, which occurred on May 11, 1779, the following declaration was found in his Last Will and Testament:

> [T]hanks be given unto Almighty God therefore, and knowing that it is appointed for all men once to die and after that the judgment [Hebrews 9:27] . . . principally, I give and recommend my soul into the hands of Almighty God who gave it and my body to the earth to be buried in a decent and Christian like manner . . . To receive the same again at the general resurrection by the mighty power of God.[13]

Abraham Clark

During the Revolutionary War, America lost more soldiers as prisoners of war than on the battlefields. The worst British prison ship was the hell ship *Jersey*, where filth, disease, and starvation claimed the lives of more than eleven thousand American soldiers. When a prisoner died in those sordid confines, the corpse was simply thrown overboard, evidenced by the shores of Long Island, which became white with human bones.

When the British stormed New Jersey, Abraham Clark's two sons, Thomas and Isaac, were captured and sent to the *Jersey*. They had enlisted without patronage or favor and consequently served on the front lines. When the astonished enemy discovered that those two young patriots were sons of a signer of the Declaration of Independence, they were immediately segregated and brutalized. They were thrown into the darkest of dungeons and sometimes were denied food for days. Great Britain eventually offered to release the boys if Abraham Clark would renounce the Declaration. His response was "If I did that it would be a lie . . . so I can not. I believed in it then and I believe in it now." Abraham Clark was the epitome of integrity. Thomas and Isaac Clark were eventually released through the efforts of George Washington.

Abraham Clark was born on February 15, 1726, in Elizabethtown, New Jersey. He grew up an only child on the farm of his parents. As the farmhand of his father, his responsibilities were great, and although he studied hard, his education was neglected. His slender stature made it obvious to everyone that the rigors of farm life would not suit him, so he turned his interest to full-time studies. In time, he became adept at surveying and law. Because he had no formal legal education, he was limited to handling less complicated tasks, such as recording deeds and mortgages—mostly for folks who could not afford higher counsel. He soon became known as the Poor Man's Counselor.

In 1749, Abraham married Sarah Hatfield, from a well-to-do family of Essex County. Sarah was related to General Matthias Ogden[aw] and Governor Aaron Ogden.[ax] The happy couple—and eventually their ten children— settled into their community and became well-liked and respected members. With his popularity, Abraham Clark became the county clerk and sheriff of Essex County, positions he held until Great Britain became aware of his republican views.

After hostilities with the Crown erupted, Clark joined the Provincial Committee of Public Safety, where he displayed sound leadership. He also demonstrated a strong and determined work ethic and a high degree of morality—far beyond the average. In 1776, he was elected to the Continental Congress, where he became the unofficial leader of the freshman delegates. Like his fellow compatriots from New Jersey, he knew that by signing the Declaration of Independence, he was risking his life and personal property. Although fate would spare his life and property, his boys endured much hardship for his patriotic actions. With the exception of one term, he stayed an active and productive member of Congress until peace was reached.

In 1783, Clark returned home, where he concentrated on state government as a member of the legislature. In that capacity, he was forced

---

[aw] Matthias Ogden (brigadier general in the Continental Army, 1754–1791) fought alongside Generals Montgomery and Arnold at Quebec.

[ax] Aaron Ogden (governor of New Jersey, and soldier in the Continental Army, 1756–1839) was the younger brother of General Mathias Ogden. He fought and was wounded at the Battle of Yorktown. In 1812, he was elected governor of New Jersey.

to deal with the deficiencies and inequities of the Confederation. He was among the first to recognize the many defects contained in the Articles of Confederation and was one of the first delegates to be elected to the Constitutional Convention, where those defects were to be corrected. When the new Constitution was ratified and the new government organized, he was elected to the first congress and continued to be active until he retired from public life in June 1794.

A few months later, at sixty-eight, Abraham Clark died from sunstroke and was buried in the churchyard in Rahway, New Jersey. He was remembered as a warm partisan who dedicated his life to the service of his constituents and his county.

Richard Stockton

Richard Stockton was a man of principle and always stood on the side of freedom, as evidenced by his stance on both the abolition of slavery and British tyranny. He sacrificed everything for his high ideals, including his life. He was one of the nine signers who died without seeing America's freedom.

The Presbyterian ancestors of Richard Stockton immigrated to America from England between 1660 and 1670 and settled on Long Island. His grandfather, a man of substantial means, later purchased a fine piece of property near Princeton, New Jersey. Part of that land was donated to establish the University of New Jersey, which eventually became Princeton University. The remainder of the property became the family seat and was named Morven. It was the birthplace of Richard Stockton, who was born on October 1, 1730. Young Richard showed incredible intellectual skills and sailed through all his educational endeavors, graduating from Princeton at eighteen. Soon after, he began the study of law under the Honorable David Ogden[ay] of Newark.

[ay] David Ogden (judge, speaker of the New Jersey General Assembly, 1726–1801) sided with the colonies when the Revolutionary War broke out.

Stockton was admitted to the bar in 1754. While there, his talents were so demonstrated that within nine years, he was awarded the status of sergeant-at-law, the highest distinction in the courts of England. Several of the Founding Fathers studied law under Stockton, including William Paterson, Joseph Reed, and Elias Boudinot, who later became the ninth president of the Continental Congress and signed the peace treaty with Great Britain. Elias and Richard eventually enjoyed another connection—they became brothers-in-law—twice. Richard married Elias's sister, Annis Boudinot, and Elias married Richard's sister, Hannah Stockton. In 1762, Richard and Annis embarked upon their domestic journey at Morven. That grand manor would eventually be filled with their six children: two sons and four daughters.

The fame of Richard Stockton spread not only throughout the colonies, but also across the Atlantic. In the latter part of 1766 and most of 1767, he made a tour of England, where he was the guest of the most notable men in the realm, including the king. He furthered his learning by attending their high courts of law, where great legal minds such as Sir William Blackstone argued their cases. It was also during that trip that he met with and attempted to recruit Reverend John Witherspoon—probably the most influential teacher in the history of American education—to relocate to America and assume the presidency of Princeton University. The following is an excerpt from Stockton's letter of introduction to the Reverend: "A Gentleman of Fortune and Figure in his Profession of Law, of distinguished Abilities, & Influence here, and a warm Friend to the interests of Religion and Learning."[14]

In 1774, just as the Boston port was being closed, Stockton reached the pinnacle of his legal career by being appointed to the New Jersey Supreme Court. With that kind of fame, ample fortune, and comfortable life, it would have been easy for him to try to preserve all that he had by remaining loyal to the Crown—or at least neutral. Instead, this patriot would not allow self-interest to govern his principle, and he ended up risking everything for the freedom of the colonies. By that time, Morven had become a meeting place for some of the greatest patriots of the day, so it was not surprising that when the Continental Congress met to declare their independence, Stockton was among the New Jersey delegates. He was firm on his pursuit for liberty, but had doubts about whether full independence was a realistic option. Just prior to the momentous vote and after hearing John Adams's plea, he was convinced that principle must rule, even over insurmountable odds. After signing the Declaration, he returned home, where he was elected chief justice of New Jersey.

Late in 1776, as the Royal Army began to advance into New Jersey with the same swath of destruction that they had doled out in New York, Stockton was able to be of direct service to General Washington. While the commander was retreating and attempting to stay ahead of the British forces, Stockton used his own resources to feed, clothe, and supply shelter for the Continentals. Once Washington had moved on and after the rear guard had vanished from sight, Stockton's concern turned to his family. Knowing they were in jeopardy, he gathered them together, along with a few belongings, and fled to a safe house in Monmouth County, a distance of about thirty miles.

Once his family was secure, he returned to Princeton for an important defense meeting at the home of a fellow patriot. Later that night, a Loyalist neighbor who had recognized Stockton betrayed him into the hands of the British authorities, who immediately arrested him. During the arrest, Stockton was beaten, stripped, robbed, tossed over a horse, and delivered to the worst dungeon his captors could find. Because he was one of the "ringleaders of the rebellion," he was treated with special vengeance, often subjected to beatings and left for days without food. It was in that belly of the prison that the disease that soon claimed his life would take root. The British did not stop with the assault on his person, but also ravaged his beautiful mansion, burned his law library and personal papers, and consumed his livestock—most of which were of the finest pedigree.

News of Stockton's capture and atrocious treatment first reached Congress on January 3, 1777. Congress immediately ordered General Washington to send a flag to General Howe for the purpose of investigating the allegations. When the report proved factual, Washington threatened his British counterpart with retaliation on Loyalist citizens, which prompted a prisoner exchange. Shortly thereafter, Stockton was freed, but he had been completely debilitated. He was never able to recover from his cruel and brutal treatment, or pick up the pieces of his shattered life. On February 28, 1781, at age fifty, after several years of continual decline of his health, Richard Stockton's life ended. Stockton's family survived the Revolution and furnished America with a number of distinguished citizens. In 1951, New Jersey selected Morven as the state's official governor's mansion. In his Last Will and Testament, he stated,

> I think proper here, not only to subscribe to the entire belief of the great leading doctrine of the Christian religion … but also in the heart of a father's affection, to charge and exhort them to remember "that the fear of the Lord is the beginning of wisdom."[15]

George Taylor

In 1776, the delegation from Pennsylvania that attended the Continental Congress had a few members who were opposed to independence. That opposition was typical of Pennsylvania politics and was more than just Whigs versus Tories. First, Pennsylvania had a large Quaker population, morally opposed to fighting, so they were usually neutral. Second, the Philadelphia economy relied heavily on trade with Great Britain, so that segment of the population leaned Tory. Lastly, the frontier dwellers who lived in the western part of Pennsylvania were extremely independent in their thinking. They were self-reliant, and they felt that they were a long way from the reach of the British, so they were natural Whigs.

In June, after Richard Henry Lee's resolution had been debated, the Pennsylvania contingent voted negative. Ross was absent (at home attempting to seize control of the state assembly for the Whigs), Franklin and Wilson were *yea*, while Morton, Morris, Dickenson, Humphreys, and Willing were *nay*. The July 1 vote produced the same outcome. However, the next day, when it appeared that the other twelve colonies were ready to support independence, patriotism overruled their reluctance to support the resolution. For the July 4 vote, Robert Morris and John Dickenson were purposely absent, reducing the quorum to five. Then John Morton joined

Benjamin Franklin and James Wilson, which swayed the Pennsylvania vote to the affirmative. More importantly, that shift allowed Congress to unanimously support the Declaration of Independence—a strong and unified statement to the American citizenry, to the colonial forces, as well as to the Crown.

The aftermath of those events was substantial. The two who were opposed, Humphreys and Willing, were removed, and Dickenson, a Quaker, resigned. Morris was allowed to remain because he explained that he was never really against independence; he had felt that the resolution was premature. His patriotism was never questioned. On July 20, the three vacancies were filled with four new delegates: George Clymer, Benjamin Rush, James Smith, and George Taylor. With the four new delegates replacing the three departing delegates, the Pennsylvania delegation had a total of nine members, the largest state contingent at Congress.

George Taylor was born in Ireland in 1717 and was raised in a Christian home. His father, even though a poor clergyman, was able to arrange an excellent education for young George. When he was but a teenager, he left home and set sail for America, the land of opportunity. Having very little money, he boarded the ship as a redemptioner, one for whom the ship's captain would have the right to be reimbursed for the cost of the passage directly from a prearranged employer in America. Upon his arrival, George agreed to work for Durham Ironworks, a Philadelphia-based company. Mr. Savage, the owner of the ironworks company, paid the redemption money, obligating the lad to work for him for a specific number of years.

Because George was tall and had a sturdy frame, it was determined that he would be a filler, one who shovels coal into the furnaces. After a short time, it was discovered that he was not the typical laborer. He possessed superior intellect, was well educated, and would be better suited for the accounting room. In his new capacity, he performed well and became a most valued employee.

For many years, George labored and eventually learned every aspect of Durham Ironworks. Then in 1738, Savage died, leaving his business to his young widow, Nancy. She knew very little about the operations and asked George to stay on as the manager. He agreed to the new position, but got much more than he had bargained for. A year later, a romance between the two began, which culminated in marriage. At twenty-three, George Taylor became the sole operator of the company. In 1764, after accumulating a great deal of wealth and respect, he moved to Northumberland County with his wife and two children. Once there, he bought a tract of land on the Lehigh River, where he built a huge stone mansion and established an ironworks company.

During the same year, Taylor was elected to the Colonial Assembly, where he was very active in supporting the issues important to his community. The following year, after the passage of the Stamp Act, he was selected as a delegate to represent Pennsylvania at the General Colonial Congress, a forum in which the colonies could consult and support each other for their common well-being. Taylor was so well respected that he was asked to pen the articles by which all delegates would conduct themselves. Over the next five years, he remained a constant participant at that congress. Finally in 1770, he returned to his home and business, both of which had suffered from neglect during his absence.

In early July 1776, George Taylor was appointed to be one of the replacements for Pennsylvania's congressional delegation. Taylor arrived in Philadelphia on July 20. On August 2, he answered his country's call once more by stepping forward and placing his signature on the Declaration of Independence. Although he had not voted for independence, he eagerly endorsed it. He remained in Congress for another year before retiring. During the Revolution, he also supported the army by using his ironworks company to turn out vast quantities of shot and other munitions of war. George Taylor died on February 23, 1781, at the age of sixty-three, never witnessing the fruition of America's pursuit of liberty.

Benjamin Rush

In the middle of July 1776, Pennsylvania chose four replacement delegates for the Continental Congress. One of those replacement delegates was the beloved Dr. Benjamin Rush, one of the leading citizens of the state. He arrived at Carpenters' Hall too late to vote for independence, but early enough to sign that glorious parchment that birthed the United States. Rush had been offered a seat at Congress in 1775, but declined the honor, choosing instead to continue serving his patients through his medical practice. However, when Pennsylvania asked a second time—during Congress's time of need—he accepted the call.

John Rush, the great-great-grandfather of our subject, was born in England in 1620. He is noteworthy due to his service to Oliver Cromwell, Lord Protector of the Commonwealth of England, Scotland, and Ireland. He served as an officer in Cromwell's army. Sometime during the latter part of the seventeenth century, he became a Quaker and later immigrated to America in search of religious freedom. In 1683, he packed up his children and grandchildren and sailed for Pennsylvania.

William Rush, John's son, was born in Broughton, England in 1652. He was twenty-nine when he arrived in Pennsylvania with his father. William's son, James, also was born in England (in 1679) and accompanied his father and grandfather to Pennsylvania. The entire Rush clan settled in Berberry, a town located approximately twelve miles north of Philadelphia. For his livelihood James—Benjamin's grandfather—took up farming and also became a gunsmith. James Rush's son, John, was born on the family farm in 1712 and, like his father, he also became a farmer and gunsmith. In the 1730s, John married Susanna Hall—Benjamin was their fourth child (of seven).

Benjamin Rush was born on December 24, 1745, at the family farm in Berberry. At age six, his father died, leaving his mother to cope with all the intricacies of a large family: managing the farm, handling the finances, raising the children, providing for their education, and so on. Much of those burdens fell on Benjamin and his brother. After two years of struggling, Susanna realized that their small farm could not supply the financial means needed to adequately provide for her children, and especially for the education of Benjamin, who appeared to possess a great aptitude for learning. Susanna sold the farm, moved to Philadelphia, began a small but successful mercantile enterprise, and sent young Benjamin off to Nottingham, Maryland, to live with his maternal uncle, where he could receive a classical education. Reverend Dr. Samuel Finley,[az] Benjamin's uncle, was the headmaster of a school—that school eventually became the West Nottingham Academy.

In 1759, after five years under Finley's instruction, Benjamin completed his preparatory schooling. With his mother's business doing well, the finances were such that young Benjamin could attend the college of his choice. He chose Princeton. Breezing through his undergraduate studies, he graduated with a bachelor of arts degree before the end of 1761—he was only sixteen. The profession of law was Benjamin's first choice, but after consulting with Finley, he decided to pursue medicine. Over the next five years, he apprenticed under the acclaimed Dr. John Redman in Philadelphia. In 1766, with his apprenticeship complete, he sailed for England so that he might expand his knowledge and polish his medical skills. After two years of additional study, attending lectures, and interning in some of London's

---

[az] Samuel Finley (founder of West Nottingham Academy, fifth president of Princeton University, 1715-1766) became the president of Princeton University in 1761. After his death in 1766, John Witherspoon succeeded him as sixth president of Princeton.

finest hospitals, he traveled to Paris for the purpose of broadening his general education. While there, he became fluent in French, Italian, and Spanish—and more culturally refined. In 1769, at the age of twenty-four, Benjamin returned to America bearing the credentials of doctor of medicine, which he earned at Edinburgh University.

Upon his return to Philadelphia, Benjamin Rush launched his own medical practice. In the years to follow, his bedside manners, superior knowledge, cordial nature, and heedfulness of the poor caused his practice to flourish. With the intent of elevating his profession, he held regular lectures, which were attended by professionals and medical students[ba] from all over the colonies. Even the most elite practitioners in Philadelphia would occasionally seek him out for consultations. Benjamin Rush had become one of Pennsylvania's favorite sons.

When Dr. Rush left Europe and returned to the colonies, there was a marked difference in his political views—he became a Whig activist. Many other young colonists, who had been raised in America but partially schooled in Europe—where they were exposed to Europe's superior attitude and hierarchical views—demonstrated the same phenomenon. With that theory in mind, it is supposed that Rush's patriotic sentiments were formed—or at least heightened—during his years in Europe. Whatever the cause, once Rush was back on Pennsylvania soil, he immediately put his pen to work, writing essays and editorials that were considered pro-independence. In 1773, Rush joined the Philadelphia chapter of the Sons of Liberty. He even collaborated with Thomas Paine in the writing of *Common Sense*. Through his writings he persuaded many to get active in the colonial cause.

In August 1775, Dr. Rush visited his alma mater, Princeton University, and while there he met Richard Stockton's daughter, Julia. Benjamin began courting her, which resulted in their marriage five months later. Julia and the doctor eventually had thirteen children, three of whom did not survive infancy.

Benjamin Rush lent his exalted status to the Continental Congress when he took his seat in that body just prior to the August 2 signing ceremony. After signing the Declaration, Dr. Rush stayed in Congress and served on

---

[ba] One of Benjamin Rush's contemporary biographers claimed that, through his private tutoring and his lectures, he gave instruction to more than two thousand pupils during his career.

the Medical Committee. A few months later, that post took him to George Washington's camp on the Pennsylvania shores of the Delaware. Dr. Rush's medical services were needed after the Continental Army's disastrous stand in New York and their subsequent retreat through New Jersey. There were many sick and wounded soldiers who were in need of medical attention. It was during that stint on the front lines of the War of Independence that Rush attended a council of war meeting with Washington and his officers for the purpose of planning an offensive strike on Trenton. Dr. Rush remained with the army during its assault on Trenton and Princeton, and he suffered with the troops through part of the frigid winter in Morristown. He was back in Congress by February 1777, where later that spring he was appointed physician general of the middle division of the Continental Army. He was soon after dispatched to the military hospitals at Princeton, where he remained for almost a year.

During his time working in the military hospitals—and seeing firsthand the high number of casualties, epidemics of typhoid and yellow fever, lack of medical supplies, as well as other illnesses affecting the soldiers—he couldn't help but notice the disarray of the medical services being administered to the soldiers. In the following year, Dr. Rush put his pen to work for the military. He wrote and published a manual for the medical treatment of the soldiers. His work was titled *Directions for Preserving the Health of Soldiers*. His manual was used by the military for the next century. He spent the next few years consumed with his private practice and delivering medical lectures at the University of Pennsylvania.

In 1783, with the war for American independence over, he joined the staff of Pennsylvania Hospital, a relationship that he maintained until his death. With his position at the hospital, he had time to pursue some of his other interests, which included: securing the charter for Dickenson College, at Carlisle, Pennsylvania (1783); being a founding member of the Philadelphia Dispensary for the Poor (1786); being a founding member of the College of Physicians of Philadelphia (1787); and being elected an officer of the Pennsylvania Society for Promoting the Abolition of Slavery (1787). He also published many policy papers and essays on various subjects that were dear to him.

Once the Constitutional Convention concluded and a new federal Constitution was adopted, it needed to be ratified by the states before becoming the organic law of the land. To facilitate this next step in Pennsylvania, a state convention was convened. Rush was elected a delegate to that body and attended the daily debates between November 21 and December 15, 1787. He was a proponent of the Constitution and led the battle for its ratification in Pennsylvania. Two years later, he and James Wilson teamed up to rewrite the Pennsylvania constitution so that it was consistent with the federal Constitution.

When the yellow fever epidemic descended on Philadelphia in 1793, it claimed thousands of lives. Dr. Rush's loyalty to his state and his profession was truly impressive. Many other doctors fled[bb] the city to save themselves and their families, but Dr. Rush and a few of his committed pupils stayed and administered medical services to the sick and dying. While making his plea to his pupils, Dr. Rush said,

> As for myself, I am determined to remain. I may fall a victim to the epidemic, and so may you, gentlemen. But I prefer, since I am placed here by Devine Providence, to fall in performing my duty. If such must be the consequence of staying upon the ground, than to secure my life by fleeing from the post of duty . . . I will remain, [even] if I remain alone.[16]

Dr. Rush was severely attacked by the fever, but survived. Sadly, some of his pupils did not.

President John Adams appointed Dr. Rush to be treasurer of the US Mint in 1797. He held that appointment for the remainder of his life, even though his tenure overlapped the terms of the next two presidents. During the latter part of his life, Dr. Rush also held three professorships: professor of the Institutes of Medicine and of Chemical Science at the Medical College of Pennsylvania; professor of the theory and practice of medicine at the College of Philadelphia; professor of the Institutes and Practices of Medicine at the University of Pennsylvania.

Dr. Benjamin Rush enjoyed the vitality of his life until his end, which occurred on April 19, 1813, after a short illness. He was sixty-seven. During

---

[bb] It has been estimated that twenty thousand citizens (out of a total population of fifty thousand) fled Philadelphia to escape the yellow fever. The fever claimed five thousand lives.

the few days that preceded his passing, thousands of people were praying for him, and well wishes were sent to him from every part of the state. When the news of his death was released, a melancholy shadow fell over the entire country—there was universal mourning. It was said of his passing that only Washington and Franklin were lamented more.

His contemporary biographer summed up his life as follows:

> As a patriot, Doctor Rush was firm and inflexible; as a professional man he was skillful, candid, and honorable; as a thinker and writer, he was profound; as a Christian, zealous and consistent; and in his domestic relations, he was the center of a circle of love and true affection. Through [his] life the Bible was a "lamp to his feet"—his guide in all things appertaining to his duty toward God and man.[17]

George Ross

Aclose connection exists between Francis Hopkinson (New Jersey) and George Ross, one of the Pennsylvania signers. They both had joint involvement in the creation of the first official American flag. The multitalented Francis Hopkinson initially designed the flag. He envisioned the newly declared United States as a new constellation in the heavens—hence, the thirteen stars on a midnight-blue backdrop. The thirteen red and white stripes would signify the blood that would be spilled by each state—the cost of liberty. George Ross, a good friend of Hopkinson, then commissioned Betsy Griscom Ross, his niece by marriage, to sew the flag. Betsy may have had some input into the shape (a circle) of the constellation. Congress approved the new flag on June 14, 1777. George Ross also was related by marriage to two other signers: James Wilson of Pennsylvania and George Read of Delaware.

George Ross was born in 1730 in New Castle, Delaware. He was the son of a highly esteemed Episcopalian clergyman. He was one of eleven children, many of whom figured prominently during America's struggle for freedom. His father, the benefactor of a good and thorough Christian education, likewise made sure that young George received a classical[bc] education. George excelled in all subjects and became proficient in Greek and Latin. Having completed his preparatory schooling at eighteen, George entered the study of law. He apprenticed at the law office of his brother, John Ross, who was a prominent member of the Philadelphia bar and a good personal friend of Benjamin Franklin. At age twenty-one, he completed his studies and began his own practice in Lancaster, his place of residence.

During that same year, George married Ann Lawler, a beautiful and accomplished young woman. The union was considered highly advantageous for both. Three children were born to them: George, James, and Mary. They were fostered to become staunch patriots. In fact, in 1775, James raised the first regiment in Lancaster County and became its captain. He was eventually promoted to the rank of lieutenant colonel.

In 1768, George Ross was elected a member of the Pennsylvania Assembly, marking his entrance into the public arena. He was well respected in that capacity and was reelected several terms in succession. As Great Britain's acts of oppression became magnified, men of leadership were pressured to choose sides. They embraced either the Crown or republicanism.[bd] Ross espoused the colonial cause, recommending and proposing the call for a provincial general congress to discuss and debate those issues and to decide whether or not to send a delegation to Philadelphia. Once his proposal was approved and the general congress met, they chose delegates to attend the Continental Congress—Ross was chosen to be one of those delegates. As a testimony to his esteemed reputation within the Pennsylvania Assembly, he was directed to devise the articles that would govern the congressional delegation.

[bc] A colonial "classical education" was founded on the trivium, a Latin word that refers to three paths of learning (grammar, logic, and rhetoric). The early American educators taught logic to their students so that they could reason analytically and not be misled by deceptive arguments. Rhetoric taught students to write expressively and to convey information accurately and persuasively. For more information, see the profiles of Peyton Randolph and Thomas Jefferson.

[bd] Republic: a state in which the exercise of the sovereign power is lodged in representatives elected by the people (*American Dictionary of the English Language* by Noah Webster, 1828). Republicanism: attachment to a republican form of government (*American Dictionary of the English Language* by Noah Webster, 1828).

Ross held that seat consecutively for three years, except for a brief absence during the vote for independence, when he was at home attempting to seize control of the state assembly for the Whigs. He simultaneously held both his state assembly seat and his congressional seat, both without pay. In fact, out of appreciation for his service, Lancaster County offered him a gift of 150 pounds of sterling silver. He courteously refused the gesture, stating that it was the duty of every man "to contribute by every means within his power to the welfare of his country without expecting pecuniary rewards."[18] He returned to the Continental Congress in time to sign the Declaration of Independence.

George Ross also had a benevolent side to his character, often handling legal cases free of charge for those who could not afford to pay. As an example, he took up the cause of the displaced Indians in his vicinity and in most cases negotiated friendly agreements with the settlers. His philanthropy was not limited to the natives, but extended even to the Loyalists. During the winter of 1777, when the Continental Army was quartered in Valley Forge and the British troops were in control of the majority of Pennsylvania, the Loyalists perpetrated countless acts of treachery and cruelty against American patriots. Later, when the Royal forces vacated the area, those Loyalists were arrested. Even in that egregious situation, George Ross was willing to lend his aid and plead their cases. Although those highly principled acts were not always popular, they were considered noble, and no one ever questioned his patriotism.

In April 1779, George Ross became a judge of the Court of Admiralty for Pennsylvania, an office he held until his sudden death, which occurred one year later. In July 1780, at the age of fifty, he died from a severe attack of gout, never seeing his country's independence.

James Smith

In November 1775, the Pennsylvania Assembly met and passed a resolution prohibiting their congressional delegates from voting for independence. However, in June of the following year, the assembly lifted those restrictions. The delegates' authority to vote for independence was left ambiguous, as they were neither instructed to vote in the affirmative nor were they instructed not to. The delegates were expected to concur with the majority on the question of independence.

James Smith was from the radical west of Pennsylvania, and like most from that region, he was an early supporter of the movement for independence. When he received word of the British assault on the townspeople at Lexington—the shot heard round the world—he immediately swung into action and assembled the first Pennsylvania volunteer corps. That action spawned other companies and eventually grew into a state militia of over twenty thousand soldiers. He was so respected as a leader that he was chosen to be their commander. At the time, he was sixty-two years old, so the position was more honorary than practical.

The Irish father of this patriot immigrated to America sometime during the early 1720s when James was a young child. The year in which James Smith was born was not recorded, and being a bit of an eccentric, he could never be coaxed into telling. His tombstone indicates his year of birth to be 1720. Upon arriving in America, the family settled near the Susquehanna River in Pennsylvania. Young James received a good education, which culminated at the College of Philadelphia, where he studied under Reverend Dr. Francis Alison. He especially excelled in Latin, Greek, and mathematics, which included practical surveying. After graduating, he apprenticed in law under his older brother, an established lawyer in Lancaster.

Having completed his education, James relocated to Shippensburg, Pennsylvania, a thriving town on the frontier, where he prospered greatly as both a lawyer and surveyor. After a few years, he moved to the town of York, a more populated area, and found very little competition for his law practice. In 1746, shortly after his move, he married Miss Eleanor Armor, an accomplished woman with good family connections. Over the next few decades, James Smith prospered domestically, enlarging his family to include five children: three sons and two daughters. His law practice also prospered, and by the time the Revolution broke out, he was head of the bar.

In July 1776, when several of the Pennsylvania delegates resigned their seats at the Continental Congress due to their opposition to independence, Smith was called on to support the cause in a new capacity. He assumed one of those vacancies and reached Philadelphia in time to affix his signature to the Declaration of Independence. After independence had been declared, each state needed to establish new governments. To help facilitate Pennsylvania's, Smith was called home. Upon the establishment of his home state's constitution, he returned to Congress and was immediately appointed to a committee whose responsibility was to aid General Washington in the supervision and the operation of military movements. That appointment required not only military knowledge, but also the utmost of integrity, because the committee was entrusted with almost unlimited discretionary power.

During the revolutionary years, Smith was unselfishly dedicated to his country. He left his personal affairs to his good wife, as evidenced by the following excerpt from a letter he sent to Eleanor while he was at Congress on September 4, 1778:

You, my dear, have been fatigued to death with the plantation affairs; I can only pity but not help you . . . I have not time to finish, but you will have [had] nonsence enough, Your loving husband, whilst.

James Smith.[19]

When victory became apparent, the sixty-three-year-old patriot retired from public life. James Smith enjoyed a long retirement, living until the ripe old age of eighty-five. His death occurred on July 11, 1806. His biographer described him this way:

Mr. Smith was quite an eccentric man, and possessed a vein of humor, coupled with sharp wit, which made him a great favorite in the social circle in which he moved. He was always lively in his conversation and manners, except when religious subjects were the topics, when he was very grave and never suffered [allowed] any in his presence to sneer at or speak with levity of Christianity. Although not a professor of religion, he was a possessor of many of its sublime virtues, and practiced its holiest precepts.[20]

Caesar Rodney

T he colony of Delaware was originally settled by the Swedes and was briefly under Dutch rule. In 1681, it was included in the land grant that was issued to William Penn and thus came under Pennsylvania control. William Penn, the founder of Philadelphia, the City of Brotherly Love, allowed the lower three counties on the Delaware River to have their own legislature, subordinate to Pennsylvania's. In 1776, Delaware was finally organized into a separate colony, but its politics were always tied closely to its parent. Many of Delaware's leading men served in both provinces, so it was not surprising that Delaware, like Pennsylvania, had a split vote on independence. Delaware's assembly had placed no restrictions on their congressional delegates concerning independence. They were free to vote their conscience.

In June 1776, the Delaware representatives to the Continental Congress were Caesar Rodney, George Read, and Thomas McKean. Rodney had been present during the final debates on independence, but had been absent during the actual vote because of his military responsibilities. When the vote was ready to be taken, the two remaining delegates were split. McKean, wishing to break the tie in favor of independence, sent for Rodney, who was eighty miles away at the time. Upon receiving the message from McKean, Rodney jumped on his horse and rode all night long through rough terrain to arrive, bruised and scratched up, in time to sway the Delaware vote in favor of independence. He signed the Declaration a month later.

The ancestors of Caesar Rodney immigrated to Pennsylvania shortly after its establishment by William Penn. His grandfather later relocated to Kent County on the Delaware River, where he established a plantation. He was politically active and became very popular, holding many positions of honor and distinction in that province. His son, Caesar, preferred the quiet life of the plantation. He married the daughter of a prominent clergyman and raised a godly family. His firstborn, Caesar Rodney (our subject), received special attention to the education of his mind and heart.

Caesar Rodney was born on October 7, 1728. When his father died, young Caesar inherited not only the substantial family estate, but also the distinguished family reputation in civic leadership. He became involved with politics during his twenties and held his first major office in 1762, when he was elected to the provincial legislature.

When the encroachments of Great Britain required a for-or-against position from each pubic official, Caesar Rodney's natural choice was for the colonies, as his family had already been in America for several generations. His integrity became his hallmark, as his actions always mirrored his thoughts and words. When the Stamp Act Congress met in New York in 1765, he was unanimously elected as Delaware's representative.

He remained extremely active in politics, continuously holding his seat in the Provincial Assembly. He was eventually elevated to speaker of that body. In the summer of 1774, after Samuel Adams called for the First Continental Congress, Rodney was elected to attend. In September, he journeyed to Philadelphia, where his colleagues, Thomas McKean and George Read, joined him. After arriving and surveying the caliber of men gathered, he declared it to be "an assembly of the greatest ability" he had ever witnessed. Consistent with his nature, he took an active role. One of his early tasks was to serve on the committee that drew up the Declaration of Rights, which itemized the complaints of the colonies.

While fulfilling his congressional duties, he also was appointed brigadier general of the Delaware militia. The two posts bore heavily upon him. He was continuously traveling back and forth between his military station and Congress, but neither responsibility suffered at the expense of the other. During late 1776 and early 1777, he took leave so that he might attend to his personal affairs, which had suffered immensely from neglect. However, that reprieve did not last long, because Colonel Haslet, who had been in charge of his brigade during his absence, was killed during the Battle of Princeton. Upon receiving the news, General Rodney immediately returned to his brigade, where he soon joined up with General Washington's main army at Philadelphia and took part in the Battle of Brandywine.

Once again, political responsibilities called him off the battlefield. The call was because the people of Delaware had elected him to the highest office in the state, that of governor. He served in that capacity for four years through a time of great turmoil, a service for which the people of his state were forever grateful.

In 1782, Caesar Rodney, having witnessed his dream of a free America, retired in poor health. During his youth, he had developed skin cancer, which finally had worsened to such a point that he could no longer serve effectively. For the last ten years of his public life, he always wore a green velvet mask to hide the disfiguring effects of the disease, which had spread to his left cheek. Knowing his death was near, he calmly went home and awaited his departure to the spirit world, which took place early in 1784. He was fifty-three.

Caesar Rodney probably made the greatest sacrifice of all the signers. Prior to signing the Declaration, he was urged by family, friends, and his doctors to give up politics and seek a cure for his cancer in Europe. By staying to sign the Declaration, he knew that he was severing any chance he had for survival, but he signed anyway. For Caesar Rodney, the pledge of life, fortune, and sacred honor was not just empty rhetoric.

William Paca

The delegation from Maryland was the ninth group to be called up to the signing table. The signers from Maryland—Samuel Chase, William Paca, Thomas Stone, and Charles Carroll—were the wealthiest delegation at Congress and had more to lose financially than their counterparts. Their magnificent estates, all situated on the Chesapeake Bay, were extremely vulnerable to the Royal Navy, which patrolled the waters regularly. Fortunately for the Maryland congressional delegates, the British never attempted to occupy their colony.

Those Marylanders, unlike the state they represented, were historically courageous and determined. In 1765, when the Stamp Act was introduced, Paca and Chase, along with Carroll, vigorously opposed it. In fact, they opposed each and every attempt by Great Britain to tax without representation. Although they were zealous for independence, the people of Maryland were not. They were still hoping and praying for reconciliation with the motherland. However, on May 28, 1776, the people of Maryland remarkably changed their opinion and "ceased praying for the king and royal family!"[21] While no official resolution was passed by the state's assembly, the Maryland delegates were then free to vote their conscience and, on July 4, they voted in favor of severing the political ties with Great Britain—and later, they all signed the Declaration of Independence.

William's father was a wealthy plantation owner whose property was located on the eastern shore of Maryland. William Paca was born in 1740 at Wye Hall, the family estate. While growing up, he was afforded all the benefits of a young aristocrat, which included an excellent moral and intellectual education. He graduated from Philadelphia College at nineteen and immediately sailed for London, where he studied law at the Inner Temple for one year. After returning home, he continued the study of law at the prestigious firm of Hammond & Hall in Annapolis. There he and his future compatriot, Samuel Chase, became friends. Together, they became a most influential duo and proved to be instrumental in shaping Maryland politics. William was admitted to the bar in 1760.

During that year, he found time to get married to Mary Chew, a prominent socialite and favorite granddaughter of Samuel Chew,[be] the head of one of the oldest and most respected families in America. With William's domestic life in order, he turned his focus once again to his career, and for maximum synergy, he teamed up with his friend and political ally, Samuel Chase. The many similarities in the lives and circumstances of William Paca and Samuel Chase were eerie. Their similarities in social status, education, career, and politics have been well documented, but they also had similarities in their domestic lives. Paca, like Chase, lost his wife early in the Revolution and also was left with children to care for—he was left with five, while Chase had six. He and Chase both remarried and both fathered additional children. Paca married his second wife, Anne Harrison, in 1777.

William Paca joined the legislature in Annapolis the same year as Chase. The two genteel Marylanders were cordial, elegant, well dressed, and well spoken, and consequently they were able to influence men of all ranks. They persistently organized many public protests, openly opposed Tory politics, wrote anti-Crown pamphlets, and won the hearts of the commoners. Their patriotic stance earned them seats at the First Continental Congress. Thomas Stone joined them in 1775 and Charles Carroll in 1776.

Paca resigned from Congress in 1778 to become the chief justice of Maryland. He fulfilled that office faithfully until he was elected governor four years later. After serving as governor for one year, he retired from public life for three years to pursue some personal affairs, one of which

---

[be] Samuel Chew was the direct descendant of John Chew, who arrived in Jamestown in 1622.

was to help establish Washington College. The state of Maryland called upon his service again to help ratify the federal Constitution, and once ratified, President Washington appointed him federal judge for the district of Maryland. He held that office until his death in 1799. He was fifty-nine. His biographer described him as follows:

> A pure and active patriot, a consistent Christian, and a valuable citizen, in every sense of the word. His death was mourned as a public calamity; and his life, pure and spotless, active and useful, exhibited a bright exemplar for the imitation for the young men of America.[22]

Charles Carroll

Charles Carroll, like Benjamin Franklin, enjoyed international recognition, as he was constantly in communication with men of influence all over Europe. Prior to the start of the Revolution, a British correspondent angrily warned Carroll that if America did not stop its rebellion "six thousand English soldiers would march from one end of the continent to the other." Carroll prophetically replied, "So they may—but they will be masters of the spot only on which they camp."[23] His reply precisely described the war that would be fought, because being outnumbered, less experienced, underfinanced, and short of munitions, General Washington was forced to wage a guerrilla campaign.

After being delayed on official business, Carroll arrived at Philadelphia on July 8, 1776, too late to vote for independence, but in time to "most willingly" sign the Declaration. When Carroll—who was then considered to be the richest man in America—signed the Declaration, someone from the gallery shouted, "There goes a few million!"[24]

Daniel Carroll, the grandfather of Charles Carroll, immigrated to America from Ireland during the latter part of the seventeenth century, during a time when Catholics were victims of all kinds of persecution. His family was prominent, having held office during the reign of James II. He secured a proprietor's commission in Maryland under Lord Baltimore, who had originally established the colony as a refuge for fellow Catholics. The family plantation was established on the Chesapeake Bay and given the name Carrollton.

On September 20, 1737, Charles Carroll was born. His early education was administered under the careful tutelage of his mother. When he was eight, his father took him to France and entered him in the Jesuit College of St. Omer. His cousin John Carroll, who became the first Roman Catholic bishop in America, attended with him. He later transferred to Louis-le-Grand College in Paris, where he graduated at the young age of seventeen. For two years, he studied Roman law in the city of Bourges, followed by five years at the Inner Temple in London. He also took time for social refinement, becoming an expert swordsman and a graceful dancer. In 1765, Charles returned to America, a gentleman in every sense of the word.

His father had died in his absence and deeded him, as his eldest child, his 10,000-acre estate, making him the wealthiest man in Maryland, not to mention the most eligible bachelor. His bachelor status changed on June 5, 1768, as reported by the *Maryland Gazette*: "On Sunday evening . . . Charles Carroll, Jr., Esq., was married to Miss Darnell, an agreeable young Lady endowed with every accomplishment necessary to render the connubial state happy."[25] They eventually had seven children: six daughters and one son.

During the Stamp Act era, Charles Carroll took a keen interest in politics. He espoused the republican cause and became associated with men like Chase, Paca, and Stone. In the early 1770s, he wrote a series of articles attacking Royal prerogative and promoting democracy. He wrote his essays anonymously under the pen name "First Citizen," and when his authorship was discovered, his pristine reputation transcended all social classes, and he actually became the First Citizen of Maryland. The elections of 1773 were a deluge in favor of his patriot party. Out of gratitude, he was appointed to his first public position on the Committee of Correspondence. He was also offered a seat at the First Continental Congress, which he declined because he felt that he was more influential at home, pushing for independence.

In early 1776, Congress requested that Carroll, along with Franklin and Chase, visit Canada for the purpose of investigating the possibilities of their uniting with the rest of the colonies with their struggle for freedom from Great Britain's tyranny. The mission failed, not because the colony of Canada was loyal to England, but because of Canada's negative experience while fighting against Great Britain a decade earlier in the French and

Indian War. Upon his return, he took up a seat in Congress, a post he held until 1778.

Carroll continued in public service until he retired in 1801. During his public life, he served his state in various capacities and finally crowned his career by being elected a US senator under the new Constitution. His greatest contribution during his senatorial term was his help in framing the Bill of Rights. His retirement from civil service by no means marked the end of his productive life. He continued to pursue business enterprises, which included the establishment and opening of the first section of the Baltimore and Ohio Railroad in 1828. He died four years later, in Baltimore, at the age of ninety-five, still the richest man in America.

The closing of Carroll's life held two distinctions. At age ninety-five, "he had lived the most years and he was the last vestige that remained of that holy brotherhood [signers], who stood sponsor at the baptism in blood of our infant Republic."[26] In his Last Will and Testament, he stated, "On the mercy of my Redeemer I rely for salvation and on his merits; not on the works I have done in obedience to his precepts."[27] And he left this advice to his fledgling nation:

> Without morals a republic cannot subsist any length of time; they therefore who are decrying the Christian religion, whose morality is so sublime and pure . . . are undermining the solid foundation of morals, the best security for the duration of free governments.[28]

Carter Braxton

Virginia and Massachusetts Bay led all American provinces down the path of freedom. Both were propelled into the conflict by direct military acts of aggression perpetrated by their Royal governors. In Massachusetts, it was the Lexington and Concord violence; while in Virginia, it was the theft of the patriots' gunpowder from the Williamsburg magazine.

On April 20, 1775, the day after the attack at Lexington, Virginia's governor, Lord Dunmore, seized a vast amount of munitions that were stored at Williamsburg, an act accomplished with the help of the marines from the Royal frigate HMS *Fowey*. Incensed with the governor's actions, Patrick Henry immediately swung into action. He raised a band of volunteers and confronted the Royal troops, creating a standoff that may have been as bloody as Concord had it not been for the efforts of Carter Braxton. He arrived on the scene just in time to intervene. Braxton tactfully negotiated a compromise whereby Dunmore would be allowed to keep the munitions, as long as he paid for them—Henry and his patriot forces disbursed, but not before extracting a healthy sum of money from the Royal treasury. Although bloodshed had been averted, tranquility had not been restored. Fearing for his safety, the governor took refuge on the *Fowey*. In his absence, the House of Burgesses fell into the hands of the Whigs, effectively ending Virginia's Royal regime. A year later, the old House of Burgesses was permanently dissolved.

Carter Braxton was born on September 10, 1736, in Newington, Virginia. His father was a wealthy and highly esteemed plantation owner, and his mother was the daughter of Robert Carter, who at one time had been the president of the Royal Executive Council of Virginia. While Carter and his brother George were quite young, their parents died, leaving them a substantial fortune.

Young Carter received a fine Christian education, which culminated when he graduated from the College of William and Mary. In 1755, he married Judith Robinson, a young woman of wealth and prominent heritage. With that union, he was considered one of the wealthiest young men in Virginia. Their storybook affair tragically ended two years later, when Judith died during the birth of their second child. After her death, filled with remorse and hoping to escape his anguish, Carter traveled to England. In 1760, he returned to America. Shortly thereafter, he met, courted, and eventually married Elizabeth Corbin, who, like his first wife, was a woman of notable colonial heritage. They enjoyed many years of marital bliss, which was evidenced by their brood of sixteen children.

With his many influential family connections and his tremendous wealth, Carter Braxton was considered among the aristocracy, however, he disregarded his birthright and espoused republicanism. His first appearance in public life was in 1765, when he was elected to the House of Burgesses just in time to witness Patrick Henry's eloquent defeat of the Stamp Act. Over the next several years, the Burgesses fell into the hands of the Whigs and were eventually dissolved by Lord Botetourt.[bf] Immediately after that event, the Whigs all met privately and signed a non-importation agreement in protest of British tyranny. Braxton was among those patriots. In 1774, under similar circumstances when Lord Dunmore dissolved the assembly, he again demonstrated his patriotism by joining the eighty-nine members who met and established a new state assembly, a body that later elected delegates to the First Continental Congress.

In 1775, Braxton was sent to the Continental Congress to fill the vacancy caused by the death of Peyton Randolph. He was in favor of independence, and the following year, when the issue was put to vote, he backed it and later signed the Declaration. A short while after, he returned to the Virginia

---

[bf] Lord Botetourt died late in 1770 and was succeeded by Lord Dunmore.

legislature, where he served until 1785. From that time until his death in 1797, he served on and off as a member of the Virginia Council. His death occurred on October 10 of that year, at the age of sixty-one.

Carter Braxton, while not considered one of the fiery spirits of the Revolution, was a firm individual whose graceful and flowing oratory persuaded many in the direction of independence. His biographer wrote of him, "In public, as well as in private life, his virtue and morality were above reproach, and as a public benefactor, his death was widely lamented."[29]

George Wythe

W hen petitions to Parliament and the king proved ineffective and alternative means for securing America's rights were needed, Virginia replaced three of their conservative congressmen with a more spirited lot. The substitutes were Francis Lightfoot Lee, Thomas Jefferson, and George Wythe. Wythe was one of the most highly esteemed legal minds in America. His disciples included the likes of Thomas Jefferson, James Monroe, James Madison, Henry Clay, John Marshall, and James Wilson. Jefferson described him as a "model of future times."[30] Wythe declared, along with Richard Henry Lee, that the king had abdicated his authority. That theory, coming from him, carried tremendous weight in Congress. While most delegates knew in their hearts that independence was right for the colonies, Wythe's theory helped everyone make the intellectual transition.

Virginia's legislature was the third—after North Carolina and Massachusetts—to pass resolutions in favor of independence. The instructions they sent with their three new congressional delegates were more aggressive than those of other colonies up to that date. On May 17, 1776, after receiving a request from Lee, the Virginia Assembly instructed its delegates "to pursue the most effectual measures for the Security of America,"[31] freeing them to vote for independence. And that they did.

George Wythe was born in Elizabeth County in 1726. The Wythes were well-established colonials, having immigrated to Virginia during the late seventeenth century. George's parents were wealthy, and as such, he was afforded an excellent education. His mother, who was left to manage all family affairs after her husband's untimely death, supervised his studies. She was well educated and a strict Christian of the Quaker faith and thus able to personally teach Latin and Greek to young George, as well as aid him in the study of the classics. He completed his education at the College of William and Mary, where he studied law. He was admitted to the bar in 1746, at only twenty.

Before George's twenty-first birthday, death claimed his mother. Due to the prevailing law of primogeniture,[bg] the family's vast estate fell to his older brother. Her death devastated George, as he had been very close to her. Filled with despair, grief, and mourning—and trying to forget about his great loss—he fell into a life of revelry and self-gratification. That lifestyle continued for about ten years until a young woman named Ann Lewis came into his life and replaced the void caused by his great loss with an abundance of love. She also was able to redirect his self-destructive pursuits. Miss Lewis's father was a wealthy and eminent lawyer who no doubt opened many career doors for George.

Shortly after his marriage in 1756, George Wythe established his own law practice in Williamsburg and pursued his career as one anxious to make up for lost years. At about that time, his brother died, leaving him as the sole beneficiary of the Wythe fortune. Due to his superior legal talents and his patriotic stance, he rapidly gained the respect and full confidence of his community. Although his professional life was stable, Wythe's personal life was again rocked with personal tragedy. His only child died during infancy, followed shortly after by the death of his beloved wife. Alone once more, he found solace by plunging into his career and public service.

[bg] Law of primogeniture: the birthright of the firstborn son to the same parents. The firstborn son shall have the right to inherit his father's entire estate. With Great Britain's Royal family, the eldest son is entitled by primogeniture to the throne.

In 1768, Wythe was elected mayor of Williamsburg and later became a member of the House of Burgesses. His political sentiments aligned him closely with patriots such as Patrick Henry, Richard Henry Lee, and George Washington. In 1775 and 1776, he was elected a delegate to the Continental Congress, where he voted for and later signed the parchment that birthed the United States of America. The part he played was invaluable. Benjamin Rush, referring to his acute legal advice, called Wythe a "profound lawyer," and John Adams described him as "one of our best men."[32]

The following year, he returned to Virginia politics, where he became speaker of the General Assembly. In that capacity, he, along with George Mason and Thomas Jefferson, was responsible for the formation of the new Virginia constitution and government. He then teamed up with Edmund Pendleton and Thomas Jefferson for the colossal task of rewriting the voluminous laws of Virginia so that they might conform to the new state constitution.

In 1777, Wythe was elevated to the bench as one of three judges of the High Court of Chancery. The following year, he was further promoted to the top judicial position in the state, that of chancellor, a seat he retained for twenty years. While occupying that high seat, he was often called upon to make decisions on the most important issues. In such cases, he always displayed tremendous integrity, in that he ruled justly. However, those decisions were not always popular. One such decision involved the question as to whether or not pre-revolutionary debts in America were collectable by Britain in the post-revolutionary era. The popular view was no, but if the ill feelings toward the debtor were set aside, the ethical ruling was absolutely yes. Wythe chose the higher ground and ruled in the affirmative.

In 1786, he was chosen as a delegate to the Constitutional Convention and later a member of the state convention for its ratification. Once the federal Constitution was ratified, he was twice elected a senator under it. One of his other honors was his appointment as professor of law at the College of William and Mary. In an act of benevolence, he established—as well as taught at—a private school that was free to those who wished to attend it. One of his pupils was the child of one of his slaves. During his declining years, remorse filled his soul as he reminisced over the "misspent days" of his youth, compelling him to leave the following advice for young people: "time once lost, is lost forever."

In June 1806, at the age of eighty, George Wythe died after being poisoned by a greedy grand-nephew. However, he lived long enough to write the boy out of his will. Prior to his death, he also emancipated his slaves, and in his Last Will and Testament, he made provision for their support.

Benjamin Harrison

B enjamin Rush, who recorded the events surrounding the signing of the Declaration, described Benjamin Harrison as one of the largest and brawniest men in Congress. Harrison was six feet four inches and weighed about 250 pounds. It was said that he could lift a full barrel by himself, normally a job for two or three men. Rush also recorded one of the only conversations that transpired during the somber event of the signing of the Declaration of Independence. It involved Benjamin Harrison and Elbridge Gerry.

> A pensive and awful silence . . . pervaded the House when we were all called up, one after another; to the table of the President [John Hancock] to subscribe, what was believed by many at that time to be our death warrants. The silence and gloom of the morning was interrupted . . . only for a moment by Colonel Harrison, of Virginia, who said to Mr. Gerry at the table: "I shall have a great advantage over you, Mr. Gerry, when we are all hung for what we are now doing. From the size and weight of my body I shall die in a few minutes; but from the lightness of your body you will dance in the air an hour or two before you

are dead!" This speech procured a transient smile, but it was soon succeeded by the solemnity with which the whole business was conducted.[33]

Both the ancestors and the descendants of Benjamin Harrison occupied prominent roles in the development of the United States. His paternal ancestor was related through marriage to the king's surveyor general and was therefore able to select some of the most fertile property in America for himself. He was among the first settlers of Virginia, having emigrated from England in 1640. He established a plantation that would remain in the family holdings for hundreds of years. Benjamin Harrison the elder, the father of our subject, was one of the most influential and wealthy landholders in the Virginia province. His wife, Anne, was also a woman of great influence. She was the daughter of the eminent Robert Carter, the speaker of the House of Burgesses and rector of the College of William and Mary.

Benjamin Harrison was born in Berkley, Virginia, on April 5, 1726. He was given an excellent Christian education at the College of William and Mary, where he thoroughly studied the classics. Prior to completing his studies, disaster fell upon his family, cutting short his education. During a violent storm, lightning struck their mansion at Berkley and killed his father and two sisters. Benjamin, the eldest of six brothers—but still a minor himself—became the owner and head of his father's great estate. Despite his young age, he fulfilled his obligations with utmost skill and fidelity, and under his stewardship, the thousand-acre plantation prospered. The family also was involved with shipbuilding and horse breeding.

Benjamin married his second cousin, Elizabeth Bassett, in 1748. The Bassett family was equally as prominent as the Harrisons, having lived in Virginia for more than a hundred years. Their union was considered beneficial for both. Benjamin and Elizabeth had eight children who survived to adulthood.

In 1749, Benjamin Harrison became a member of the Virginia House of Burgesses, where he served for twenty-five years. His leadership abilities and sound judgment had earned him the respect and confidence of his colleagues, and he was eventually elevated to Speaker of the House. The great influence that position held, along with his personal wealth and family connections, made him an important individual for the Crown to control.

At the time of the Stamp Act, the Royal governor offered him a seat in the Executive Council—a gesture meant to buy his loyalty—but Harrison was a man of utmost integrity, and his patriotism was not for sale. He boldly rejected the offer and made clear his attachments to the republican cause. That stance endeared him to the common folk.

Harrison was one of seven delegates chosen from Virginia to attend the First Continental Congress. He felt honored by the selection and embraced his responsibilities with enthusiasm. John Adams recorded that upon his arrival, Harrison stated, "He would have come on foot rather than not come."[34] While in Philadelphia, he roomed with George Washington and his brother-in-law, Peyton Randolph. He was reelected to Congress the following year and, while there, was selected to a committee whose function it was to strategize future military operations with General Washington. Later that same year, he also was appointed chairman of the Committee of Foreign Correspondence, whose responsibility was to gather military intelligence from sympathizers in Great Britain.

He remained almost constantly involved with the activities of Congress, and in 1776, when the question of independence was raised, he was chosen by Hancock to be chairman over the final debates. In that capacity, he was heralded by all as being "decisive and fair." Benjamin Rush said he was "sincerely devoted to the welfare of his country."[35] After all was debated, he favored Lee's motion and happily signed the Declaration of Independence.

The following year he resigned his seat in Congress because his private affairs demanded some attention. However, upon returning home, he was once again elected to the state assembly and immediately promoted to his usual speaker's chair, an office he held until 1782. During that time, he was also colonel of the militia and judge of the civil courts for his home county. As colonel, he labored tirelessly, along with General Thomas Nelson, to keep the militia disciplined and vigilant until the close of the hostilities, which occurred after the victory at Yorktown.

In 1782, he was elected governor of Virginia, where he served for two terms. Those were difficult times for the colonies because of the limitations of the Confederacy, problems that would not be corrected until the new federal Constitution was ratified. At the conclusion of his second term, he had hoped to retire completely from public life. However, the people of

Virginia would not hear of it and reelected him to the assembly, where he again assumed his familiar post as speaker.

In 1791, Harrison was elected governor for the third time, however, he would not live to enjoy it. The day after his election, he hosted a reception and invited many of his friends. During that evening, he suffered a fatal relapse of stomach gout, a condition that had been plaguing him for several years. He died on April 24, 1791. His seven children and wife, Elizabeth,[bh] survived him.

Benjamin Harrison established a tradition of Christianity and public servitude, which he passed down to his children and to their children. In 1841, his third son, William Henry Harrison, became the ninth president of the United States. President Harrison offered the following advice to America during his inaugural address:

> I deem the present occasion sufficiently important and solemn to justify me in expressing to my fellow citizens a profound reverence for the Christian religion, and a thorough conviction that sound morals, religious liberty, and a just sense of religious responsibility are essentially connected with all true and lasting happiness.[36]

His great-grandson, Benjamin Harrison, was the twenty-third president of the United States, serving in that office from 1889 to 1893. President Benjamin Harrison once wrote his son, Russell, the following: "It is a great comfort to trust in God—even if His providence is unfavorable. Prayer, steadies one, when he is walking in slippery places—even if things asked for are not given."[37]

[bh] Elizabeth Harrison was the niece of Mrs. Washington.

William Hooper

Opposite to the conservative stance taken by its southern neighbor, South Carolina, the citizenry of North Carolina were the first to permit their congressmen to vote for independence. On April 22, 1776, they were instructed to "concur with the Delegates of the other colonies in declaring Independency."[38] That was not a rash decision. A year earlier, the North Carolina Committees of Safety had declared themselves to be free and independent of British rule. Self-government had been the catalyst to North Carolina's existence. It had seceded from the province of Carolina and had become an independent province in 1729. North Carolina, like Georgia, had no native-born signers. Joseph Hewes was born in New Jersey, John Penn was born in the neighboring province of Virginia, and William Hooper was born in Boston.

The birth of William Hooper occurred on June 17, 1742; he was the first of his Scottish ancestors to be born in America. His father had immigrated to America as a young man shortly after graduating from Edinburgh University. He settled in Boston and soon married and began a family, of which William was the firstborn. At the time of his birth, his father was the rector of Trinity Church, so it is no surprise that his parents hoped he would take an interest in the church and eventually enter the clergy. Therefore, much attention was given to young William's education. His preparatory study was received under John Lovell,[bi] one of the most acclaimed instructors of Massachusetts Bay. William completed his schooling at Harvard University, from which he graduated with distinguished honors.

Upon graduating, William appeared better suited for the profession of law rather than the clergy. He was placed under the tutelage of James Otis, where he received his law apprenticeship. When his law studies were complete, he relocated to North Carolina, where there were fewer lawyers and more opportunity. As a result of his superior training and his success in handling a few high-profile cases, he rapidly rose to the head of the bar in Wilmington. As a high-profile lawyer, he caught the eye of the Royal governor, who took an interest in his career and began grooming him to be a man of influence in the province. Hooper eventually became deputy attorney general of North Carolina.

At about that same time, William Hooper married Anne Clark, the daughter of a prominent attorney and sister of Thomas Clark, who would later become a general in the Continental Army. Anne was a perfect choice for a man of his position, for she was a lady who possessed both social and domestic graces.

During the early 1770s, the people of North Carolina were the victims of British tyranny, suffering from acts of grossest immorality and wanton cruelty at the hands of Governor Tryon. To counter those actions, a group of patriots calling themselves Regulators rose against the governor. Mistaking them for a bunch of low-minded, rebellious malcontents, Hooper took the side of the eastern plantation owners and the Crown. He advised Governor Tryon, his client, on ways to quell the rebellion. For that act, he was labeled a Loyalist. Over time, as he pondered and assimilated the political issues, he began to openly support the cause of the colonies, based on principles that were instilled upon his heart and mind years earlier by his mentor, James Otis.

[bi] John Lovell (1710-1778) was headmaster of Boston's South Latin School. Students attending Mr. Lovell's academy were highly educated. For example, by the seventh grade, the students were able to read Cicero's orations in the original texts and language. New England, under its Puritan leadership, passed laws in 1642 mandating universal education in their colony—the first such mandates in world history. They believed that the best way to create a godly society was to equip the citizenry with a broad-based, classical education.

As Hooper continued to sympathize on the side of the oppressed, he gained the colony's confidence and eventually erased his undeserved Loyalist reputation. In 1773, he was elected to the Provincial Assembly. He was reelected the following year and became one of the most vocal opponents of the Royal government. When Massachusetts put forth the proposition for a Continental Congress, the people of North Carolina called for a convention to consider the matter. The convention approved of it and appointed Hooper, along with Joseph Hewes and Richard Caswell, as the first delegates to the Continental Congress. Although he was one of the youngest members to attend, his talents were immediately recognized, and he was placed on some of the most important committees.

In 1775, Hooper was reelected to Congress, but absent during the spring while he was attending an important meeting in Hillsborough, North Carolina. That meeting was for the purpose of putting forth an address to the people of Great Britain, the final draft of which was written from the precise and authoritative pen of William Hooper. In late May of that same year, through a series of resolutions, North Carolina declared itself free and independent of the British Crown. In support of those resolutions, the patriots who were gathered pledged their lives, their fortunes, and their sacred honor.

The following year, Hooper again returned to Congress, where the united colonies passed resolutions similar to the ones North Carolina had passed a year earlier. He heartily supported Lee's motion for independence and then enthusiastically signed the Declaration. He remained active in Congress until the spring of 1777, at which time he asked for leave to tend to his private affairs and the safety of his family. Hooper had become very offensive to the British, and they had taken every opportunity to harass his family and damage his personal property. On several occasions, the British had sailed up the Cape Fear River, about three miles from Wilmington, specifically to shell the Hooper estate. He arrived home in time to safely relocate his family.

When the war ended, he began the job of rebuilding his life, property, and law practice. He never appeared again in public office except briefly in 1786, when he was appointed a federal judge to help settle some jurisdictional disputes between Massachusetts and New York. William Hooper died in October 1790, at the age of forty-eight.

Arthur Middleton

Like Pennsylvania's mercantile trade, the South Carolina agricultural industry was closely linked with Great Britain. Consequently, the idea of trade embargoes and absolute independence was a hard concept for South Carolina to embrace. Therefore, the people of South Carolina took a stance similar to Pennsylvania's in opposition to independence. They did not vote in the affirmative until the final vote and then only out of patriotism and a desire to show unanimity.

The social and political establishments in South Carolina during the mid-eighteenth century were modeled after the English squire system, not by law, but from necessity. The gentry, professional men or successful plantation owners, were expected to be involved in local politics. The involvement was, for the most part, on a volunteer basis and was uncompensated. Socially, those elites also were expected to be gentlemen in every sense of the word. They were to have impeccable manners, perfect etiquette, and refined tastes, and be hospitable, well educated, and well dressed—an image that often irritated the Northerners. While the South's aristocratic attitudes were evident socially, they were absent democratically. The South, like the North, believed strongly that sovereignty resided in the people, not in a king or gluttonous Parliament. All four of the South

Carolina signers—Rutledge, Heyward, Lynch, and Middleton—fit the stereotype. They were all young men following their family traditions. The eldest of the foursome was Arthur Middleton.

The Middleton dynasty began in America when Edward Middleton immigrated to South Carolina and acquired a 50,000-acre land grant from the Lord's Proprietors.[bj] The elder Arthur, Edward's son, was one of the first gentry to espouse Whig philosophies. His son, Henry, built on his philosophies and became a Southern forerunner of republicanism.

Henry Middleton was born in 1717. He grew up on the family estate, which he eventually inherited, becoming one of the wealthiest planters in the South. At twenty-seven, he took a seat in the state's Common House, which he held for three years, serving as speaker during his last two terms. In 1755, he was appointed king's commissioner of Indian affairs and became a member of the South Carolina Council. He was accredited with distinguished military service during the French and Indian War, displaying exemplary leadership abilities. When the political connection with Great Britain became strained in 1774, he led the South Carolina delegates to the First Continental Congress. He was so highly esteemed in that body that when Peyton Randolph took ill, he was elected president in his stead. President Middleton, the second president of Congress, served from October 22, 1774, until Randolph returned on May 10, 1775. Early in 1776, he resigned his congressional seat so that he might prepare his estate for the inevitability of war. His oldest son, Arthur, assumed his seat and all the responsibilities that came with it. Henry Middleton never again appeared on the public stage. He died in 1784, at the age of sixty-seven.

Arthur Middleton was born in 1743 at Middleton Place, South Carolina. Young Arthur's early schooling consisted of the best moral and cultural education that the province could provide, the cost of which was never an issue. When he was twelve, he was sent to England for a thorough education, which was the prevailing custom among wealthy Southerners until just prior to the Revolution.

[bj] Lord's Proprietors: In 1660, after King Charles II regained the throne of England, he rewarded eight of his most loyal supporters by granting them massive amounts of land in America—contained in the 1663 Carolina Charter. Those eight men became the Lord's Proprietors, and they were tasked with establishing colonies within their landholdings.

After arriving in England, Arthur was placed in a preparatory school in Hackney, where he studied for a short time before transferring to Westminster. In 1758, he entered Cambridge University where, four years later, he graduated with distinguished honors. Rather than immediately returning to America, Arthur remained in England for another year so he might become more acquainted with the branch of his family that had not immigrated to America. Before his return home in 1763, he decided to further cultivate his mind by taking a thorough tour of Europe.

During the year that followed his return to South Carolina, two major events occurred in his life. First, he followed in his father's political footsteps by taking a seat in his state's colonial legislature. He held that position until 1768 and established a reputation as a true patriot. Secondly, he married Miss Mary Izard, one of the most beautiful and accomplished young ladies in South Carolina. Her father was Colonel Walter Izard, an officer of the provincial militia. She was also closely related to Lord William Campbell, who later became the Royal governor.

In 1768, Arthur packed up his family and embarked on a tour of Europe, the purpose of which was a combination of business and pleasure. Upon his return to South Carolina in 1773, he resumed his political pursuits. With the rumblings of war growing stronger, Arthur and his father committed themselves to the colonial cause, pledging their lives, fortunes, and sacred honor for the freedom of America. In 1775, the new provincial government appointed Arthur to a post on the Committee of Safety, a position he dutifully fulfilled with the utmost integrity. When it was discovered that Governor Campbell, Arthur's relative, had been acting with duplicity, he discarded all personal feelings and recommended his arrest. The committee thought that the recommendation was too bold and allowed the governor to flee the state, a decision they later regretted when Campbell allied with Great Britain and used his great influence against the patriots.

In early 1776, at age thirty-three, Arthur Middleton was sent to Philadelphia to assume his father's seat in Congress. There, he was a soft proponent for independence, and when all the arguments—for and against—had been heard, he voted in the affirmative and later signed the Declaration of Independence. He did so without giving any consideration to the fact that his property would be at risk. He remained active in Congress until 1778, when the dire situation in South Carolina required his attention.

When South Carolina was invaded by the British forces, the Middleton estate suffered severely. One of Arthur Middleton's early biographers related the following, which gives us much insight to his patriotism:

> During the Revolution when Governor Rutledge needed help in 1779, when Provost was trying to reduce Charleston, many of the patriots whose family seats lay in the route of the British, hastened home to save their property. Mr. Middleton merely sent word to his wife to remove to the house of a friend a day's journey north of Charleston. The buildings at Middleton Place were spared but house and barns rifled. Everything that could not be converted into lucrative purpose was demolished, pictures were slashed and frames broken.[39]

In all, the British confiscated over $100,000 worth of Middleton's personal property.

The following year, during the siege at Charleston, while serving in the militia with Governor Rutledge, Middleton was captured and imprisoned. He was held in St. Augustine, Florida, along with many other men of influence, such as Edward Rutledge and Thomas Heyward, Jr. Those men were offered pardons, protection, and an instant return to their opulent lifestyles if they would "change coats." They refused, choosing to suffer with the patriots rather than enjoy freedom with the Loyalists. Middleton was released in 1781 through a prisoner exchange and immediately took a seat in Congress, where he toiled until the end of the conflict.

In 1785, he was elected a representative in the state legislature, but he resigned less than two years later due to failing health. Arthur Middleton died on January 1, 1788, at the age of forty-four. He left behind his wife and eight children.

Edward Rutledge

In 1774, Henry Middleton was the head of the South Carolina delegation that attended the First Continental Congress. His accompanying delegates included Thomas Lynch, Christopher Gadsden, John Rutledge, and the lesser-known Edward Rutledge. The same contingent returned for the Second Continental Congress, but during the early part of 1776, wholesale changes were made. First, Middleton requested leave so that he might attend to some personal business. His request was granted on the condition that his son assumed his seat. The second change was similar to the first. Lynch, a strong supporter of independence, also requested leave, but his request was due to illness. His request was granted on the same condition as Middleton's—that his son would attend in his stead. The third change was that Gadsden was dropped due to the militant attitude that he had developed. After spending much of his time in Philadelphia with the likes of Adams and Lee, he vowed never to submit to Parliament's overstepping policies. Gadsden's replacement was the more conservative Thomas Heyward, Jr. Lastly, John Rutledge asked to be dismissed, as he had just been elected governor of South Carolina and wanted to give his full attention to his new high office. He was not excused, but instead listed as absent but available should the foursome ever need a tie-break. Edward Rutledge was reelected, and due to his longevity, he became the new spokesman for the South Carolina congressional delegation.

Dr. John Rutledge, the father of Edward, emigrated from Ireland to America in 1735 and settled in Charleston, South Carolina, where he established a highly successful medical practice. He immediately became welcome in the highest social circles, where his superior education, professional reputation, and successful medical practice made him one of the most eligible bachelors in South Carolina. Within a few years, he married a young lady from the Hert family, who brought a small fortune into their marriage by way of dowry.

Edward Rutledge was born in Charleston in November 1749, the youngest of seven children. After completing a traditional education, he began apprenticing law with his older brother John, who eventually became the second chief justice of the United States. When his apprenticeship was completed, he journeyed to London for the purpose of advancing his law studies. He entered as a student at the Inner Temple, where he was able to put the finishing touches on his legal education. In 1772, he returned to Charleston and joined the bar and, by the end of the year, he commenced his own law practice.

In 1774, enjoying his reputation as a brilliant young attorney with a bright future, Edward married Arthur Middleton's sister, Henrietta. She was the product of that devoutly Christian family whose patriarch was Edward Middleton.

Within a few months, Edward Rutledge was elected a delegate to the First Continental Congress, which convened in Philadelphia on September 5, 1774. He was the youngest attendee and was described by John Adams as "a young, smart, spirited body."[40] He displayed such patriotism in all his activities that he was reelected the following two years. Early in 1776, he collaborated with the likes of Richard Henry Lee and John Adams in recommending that each colony form new permanent governments. He did not, however, completely embrace independence until the final vote on July 4. In June, as leader of the conservative faction, he argued that independence was premature and that the vote should be postponed. On July 2, when the tide turned toward independence, he requested that the vote be delayed one more day, indicating that he was prepared to vote in the affirmative. He used the following day as an opportunity to negotiate some extra concessions for South Carolina and then patriotically joined the majority, notwithstanding the large numbers of constituents in his home state who opposed that decision. Later, on August 2, he fearlessly signed the Declaration of Independence. At age twenty-six, he was the youngest signer.

Rutledge's patriotism was so recognized that he was chosen to represent Congress, along with Benjamin Franklin and John Adams, in negotiating an early peace agreement with Great Britain. That negotiation occurred during the summer of 1776 on Staten Island. The three men were instructed by Congress to enter negotiations only if they were recognized as representatives of free states. That precondition was not acceptable to Great Britain, so the meeting ended without accomplishing anything important.

In 1777, Rutledge withdrew himself from Congress because of ill health and his much-neglected personal affairs. While at home, not only did he attend to his health and all his personal affairs, he also found time to take an active role in the defense of South Carolina. Two years after his departure from Congress, he returned for one last term.

The following year, as Charleston was being besieged by British troops, Rutledge returned to South Carolina. He was placed at the head of the artillery corps and was active in supplying aid to General Benjamin Lincoln. During one of his excursions, while attempting to bring more troops into Charleston, he was captured. General Cornwallis sent him to St. Augustine, Florida, where he was imprisoned for almost a year before a prisoner exchange liberated him.

When peace was effectively reached in 1781, Rutledge resumed his legal practice. After thirteen years of dividing his time between his law practice and serving in the state legislature, he was elected to the US Senate, filling the vacancy caused by the resignation of Charles Cotesworth Pinckney.[bk] He held that post for four years. In 1798, his public career was crowned when he was elected governor of South Carolina, an office he held until his death.

[bk] Charles Cotesworth Pinckney (lawyer, brigadier general in the Revolutionary War, and US senator, 1746–1825) resigned his seat in the US Senate so that he might serve in George Washington's cabinet as a diplomat.

On January 23, 1800, after a great deal of suffering from hereditary gout, Governor Rutledge caught a cold, which intensified the disease and terminated his life. He was fifty and had outlived his first wife by eight years. His son, Henry, daughter, Sarah, and second wife, Mary Shubrick Rutledge, all survived him. As a tribute to the Christian values that the governor instilled in his family, the second Mrs. Rutledge and Sarah, her stepdaughter who had never married, continued to live together after the governor's death, devoting most of their efforts to the care of the poor, as well as other charitable work. Sarah took a special interest in orphaned and homeless girls, whom she supported and educated.

Thomas Lynch, Jr.

T he new South Carolina delegation was sent to Congress with wide discretion, excepting the ability to vote for independence. However, on April 23, 1776, South Carolina's chief justice, John Drayton, delivered a speech to one of his grand juries that declared the king had abdicated American government:

> [King George III] has no authority over us, and we owe no obedience to him . . . The Almighty created America to be independent of Britain; to refuse our labors in this divine work, is to refuse to be great, a free, a pious, and a happy people.[41]

The speech evidently went a long way to having all restraints removed from South Carolina's congressional delegates.

Under the leadership of their spokesman, Edward Rutledge, they leaned toward conservatism. On July 1, the vote status on independence in Congress was as follows: South Carolina and Pennsylvania opposed, Delaware deadlocked, New York abstaining, and the rest in favor. On July 4, all states that were against independence put their hesitations aside and rallied behind the majority. History proves that the replacement delegates brought honor to South Carolina. Those delegates were Edward Rutledge, Thomas Heyward, Jr., Thomas Lynch, Jr., and Arthur Middleton. Compared with the other states' delegations, they were not typical, but as a group, they were very similar: all Anglican, all from prominent families, all very wealthy, all educated in England, and all of the same generation.

The ancestors of Thomas Lynch, Jr. were originally natives of the town of Linz, Austria. A branch of the family moved to England and settled in Kent County, and from there they relocated again to Connacht, Ireland. Jonack Lynch, the great-grandfather of Thomas Lynch, Jr., immigrated to America and purchased a large tract of fertile land in Carolina for the purpose of establishing a plantation. That tract of land was located in Prince George's Parish on the banks of the North Santee River. When Thomas Lynch, Sr. inherited that handsome estate, he became not only a man of enormous wealth, but also a man of great respect and influence. The Lynch family was among the first settlers in the province of Carolina and, therefore, possessed strong colonial patriotism—sentiments that earned Thomas Lynch, Sr. a seat at the First Continental Congress.

Thomas Lynch, Jr. was born at the family estate on August 5, 1749, where as a child he enjoyed all the fruits of one born into royalty. His early education began in Georgetown, South Carolina, and at age thirteen, he was sent to England where he was placed in a seminary school at Eton for his preparatory studies. He eventually entered the University of Cambridge, from which he graduated with highest honors. His studious and virtuous character also earned him the respect of his tutors. Before returning to America, Thomas also studied advanced law at one of the Inns of the Temple so that he might polish his legal skills, as well as his résumé.

Thomas arrived home in 1772 and soon married Elizabeth Shubrick, a beautiful young lady who had been his childhood sweetheart. They took up residence on a plantation of their own, given to them by Thomas Lynch, Sr. Being a newlywed and a possessor of ample fortune and a fine education, it would have been understandable if he had sat back and enjoyed a private life. Such would not be the case. Thomas had inherited his father's patriotic spirit and devoted his life to the advancement of the best interests of his country.

The first appearance of Thomas Lynch, Jr. on the public stage was in 1773 in Charleston during a town hall meeting, in which the topic was the encroachments of Great Britain upon the colonies. He addressed those in attendance with such patriotic eloquence that he immediately won their confidence and hearts. Over the next few years, he held many civic offices of trust and, in 1775, when South Carolina raised its first provincial regiment, he was offered the commission of captain. Lynch accepted the appointment even though his father, who was then in Congress, felt he should enter military service at a higher rank, thus escaping the front lines. In that capacity, he agreed to make a desperately needed recruiting expedition to North Carolina during some extremely inclement weather. The excursion was successful, and he raised the troops that were needed, but at the detriment of his health. His health was so compromised that he never fully recovered.

In early 1776, Lynch received word from Congress that his father had become severely ill with paralysis and had resigned his seat. Thomas Lynch was requested to replace his father. He eagerly accepted the appointment and immediately journeyed to Philadelphia, arriving in time to vote for and sign the Declaration of Independence.

The younger Lynch did not remain long in Congress because of his—and his father's—failing health. Both traveled slowly home, but before reaching their destination, the elder Lynch suffered a fatal stroke. With a bereaved heart and his own health continuing to deteriorate, Thomas Lynch completed his journey home. With the hope of restoring his health and with his physician's advice, he and his wife resolved to go to the south of Europe, where he could fully recuperate. Near the close of 1779, they sailed to the West Indies with the intent of locating a neutral ship by which they might obtain safe transportation to Europe. Their vessel never reached its destination, and it is presumed that it was lost at sea and that all on board perished. Thomas Lynch, Jr. was only thirty years old. His biographer lauded the young statesman:

> Thus, at the early age of thirty years, terminated the life of one of that sacred band who pledged life, fortune, and honor, in defence of American freedom. Like a brilliant meteor, he beamed with splendor for a short period, and then suddenly vanished forever.[42]

Lyman Hall

Georgia and Canada were the two colonies that did not attend the First Continental Congress, but for very different reasons. While Canada suffered from war fatigue and was fearful of Great Britain's wrath, Georgia felt genuinely indebted to the motherland. Beginning in the early seventeenth century, the original American colonies had been established by private adventurers who were financed primarily with private funds. Contrarily, Georgia was founded by King George II in 1752 and settled with funds from Britain's National Treasury. Therefore, most of its citizenry were reluctant to side with the other colonies in their disputes with Great Britain. However, the exception was St. John's Parish, with its great number of inhabitants of New England birth.

Dr. Lyman Hall, a prominent and leading resident of St. John's Parish, was the exception to the rule and became its leading voice against the parliamentary oppression that was being inflicted on Boston. Thus, he became the dominant patriot in Georgia. Lyman Hall was born in Wallingford, Connecticut, on April 12, 1724. His father was a man of comfortable means and afforded young Lyman a good education. At sixteen, he entered Yale College where, after four years, he graduated and became a clergyman. Meanwhile, he vigorously pursued the study of medicine and earned the title MD. In 1752, with his education behind him, he married and moved to South Carolina. Later that year, Hall, along with approximately forty other New England families (then living in Georgia), relocated to Sunbury, Georgia. The town of Sunbury was located in St. John's Parish, where he established a medical practice.

Over the next few years, he expanded his interest to that of agriculture and purchased a rice planation. In 1757, Lyman married Abigail Burr, his first wife having died only one year after their marriage. Dr. Hall was the picture of success: he had a loving wife and son, his plantation was thriving, he was highly successful in his profession, and he was greatly esteemed by his fellow citizens.

In July 1774, the Georgia Assembly called a public meeting to discuss the dire situation in New England. After lively debates, it was concluded that no action toward independence would be taken. Dr. Hall, who was the representative for St. John's Parish, returned home full of disgust for Georgia's apathetic attitude. His constituents were equally frustrated, and it was decided that their parish would make application to the South Carolina legislature to participate in their non-importation agreements. The application was unsuccessful because of South Carolina's constitutional limitations. St. John's Parish then further decided to enter into its own trade embargoes with Savannah and the rest of Georgia—not buying anything from them except for absolute necessities. They also decided to withdraw from the General Assembly, virtually seceding from the colony. The good people of St. John's Parish then sent Lyman Hall to Philadelphia as their delegate.

On May 13, 1775, Hall arrived in Philadelphia. His presence threw Congress into confusion concerning his status. By unanimous vote, it was resolved that he would be admitted to a seat, but only on the condition that he be an observer who possessed no voting rights, as votes in Congress were taken by colonies. Lyman Hall's intrepidity sparked a patriotic flame throughout Georgia that could not be doused. That, along with Britain's impolitic governing, drove Georgia to reconsider its position and send a delegation to Philadelphia.

On July 15, 1775, the Georgia Assembly officially sent Hall to the Second Continental Congress, along with a full contingent of delegates. When Lee's motion for independence was put forth, Hall fully embraced it and eventually signed the glorious document that was spawned from it. He continued to be active in Congress until 1780, when he was called home to attend to the safety of his family. He removed his family, but in so doing, he left his plantation unprotected from the invading British troops, who soon afterward confiscated his entire property. Two years later, on June 24, 1782, a few miles from Savannah, the last battle of the Revolution was fought. Cessation of hostilities was proclaimed, and the British forces evacuated Savannah, their last Georgia stronghold. Just prior to those events and after a two-year exile, Dr. Hall was able to return to his home.

In 1783, Lyman Hall was elected governor, the highest gift the people of Georgia could bestow upon him. He held the office for only one term, after which he retired from public office, except for passive duty as a county judge. The joy of the governor's well-deserved retirement did not last long. On October 19, 1790, at the age of sixty-six, the great statesman passed on to his reward. His gravestone reads:

> Beneath this stone rests the remains of the
> Hon. Lyman Hall,
> Formerly Governor of this State,
> who departed this life the 19th of October, 1790
>
> In the cause of America he was uniformly
> a patriot. In the incumbent duties of a
> husband and a father he acquitted himself
> with affection and tenderness. But, rather,
> above all, know from this inscription that he
> left the probationary scene as a true Christian
> and an honest man.[43]

Button Gwinnett

Besides the determination and courage of Lyman Hall, the loss of Georgia's loyalty to the king was rooted in Britain's ill-advised policy to inflict extreme punishment on the New England "rebels." Parliament's thinking was that they would "absolutely crush the rebellion with such severity that all other colonies would back out." However, that philosophy backfired when the other colonies perceived the Crown as a bully, one that at any time was capable of treating them in the same manner.

In early 1775, a majority of the British ministers voted in favor of arming the Indians and inciting them to besiege the colonial faithful. Georgia, a frontier colony, had seen its children tomahawked, families massacred, and men and women burned alive. They were well aware of the atrocities of which the natives were capable. Warfare like that was unheard of in the civilized European world. That policy, along with the bloodshed at Lexington, spawned sympathy from Georgians for their fellow colonists.

On July 15, 1775, the Georgia General Assembly met and voted in favor of sending a delegation to Philadelphia. Its representatives were Lyman Hall, Archibald Bulloch, John Houstoun, Noble W. Jones, and John Zubly. Their instructions were to labor for American rights and claims, but not for independence. That restriction was lifted sometime before Congress voted on Lee's resolution. When Congress's reconciliation efforts failed and a collision with the Royal forces became inevitable, the Georgia Assembly replaced several of their delegates. Those substitutions were much more spirited. In February 1776, the explosive Button Gwinnett was chosen to be one of the replacement delegates.

Button Gwinnett was born in Gloucestershire, England, in 1732. His parents, Anne and Reverend Samuel Gwinnett, were of limited means, yet arranged for an above-average education for young Button. Upon the completion of his schooling, he began an apprenticeship with a successful merchant in Bristol. When he had fulfilled his duties, he established his own mercantile business. Sometime prior to 1765, he, along with his wife and three children, immigrated to America under the allurement of wealth and distinction. Gwinnett arrived in Charleston, South Carolina, and immediately commenced his mercantile business, but after only a few years, he sold out and relocated to Georgia. He purchased an established plantation on St. Catherines Island, fully equipped with lumber, a plantation boat, and livestock—including horses and cattle.

When Great Britain began to threaten the economics of America, Gwinnett sided with the colonies. However, he was cautious because he knew firsthand the military strength of the motherland. In 1774, a contingent from the Continental Congress met with Georgia's General Assembly to coax them to join the other colonies in Congress. Gwinnett was opposed to sending a delegation to Congress, as was most of his state. However, the following year, under the influence of patriots like Dr. Hall, Gwinnett changed his attitude and lent his credibility, cultured mind, and superior talents to the colonial cause.

In 1776, he attended Congress and was present during the debates over independence. In accordance with his sentiments, he voted for and later signed the Declaration of Independence. He remained a part of that body until 1777, at which time he returned to Georgia to assist in the framing of a new constitution for his state, a task that was recommended by Congress. The Georgia Assembly chose Gwinnett as its speaker. In that capacity, he proved to be very influential during the debates and the eventual adoption of the new state constitution. Shortly after the establishment of the new constitution, Archibald Bulloch, the recently elected governor, died. The Assembly's Executive Council then elevated Gwinnett to his vacant seat.

Button Gwinnett's political rise had been phenomenal. In less than a decade, he had become a new resident, converted his natural Tory principles to that of republicanism, led all native-born Georgians in their struggle for independence, and finally had become governor. However, along the way, he had created some local enemies and excited their jealousies. One such case involved Colonel Lachlan McIntosh, who had competed against Gwinnett for the position of brigadier general during the time he was serving in Congress. Their dislike for each other grew until finally Gwinnett challenged McIntosh to a pistol duel—a British practice that was acceptable in all colonies except New England. They met, and after a single shot from each, Gwinnett was fatally wounded. He died at the age of forty-five, after suffering for twelve days with a shattered hip.

When Gwinnett had made his decision to step forward and be counted with the patriots, he prophetically stated that his stance would result in his family's ruin. He knew that St. Catherines Island was indefensible, but even knowing that, he did his duty and accepted his election to Congress. His prediction proved correct. The Loyalists confiscated his plantation and displaced his wife and children. His family survived him, but not for long, due to the hardships of war.

George Walton

The original Georgia congressional delegation included Lyman Hall, Archibald Bulloch, John Houstoun, Noble Jones, and the unscrupulous John Zubly. Of the five, Hall, Bulloch, and Houstoun were considered Whigs, while the other two were conservatives. Zubly, faced with a shift toward independence in Congress, turned Loyalist and wrote a letter betraying some congressional secrets to the Royal governor of Georgia. Samuel Chase intercepted a copy of the letter and accused Zubly of treason. Zubly immediately fled. In vain, Houstoun gave chase with the intent of apprehending him for trial.

In light of those problems and the growing sympathy for their New England neighbors, the Georgia Provincial Congress elected two new delegates. Button Gwinnett and George Walton were chosen to replace Jones and Zubly. Bulloch was called home to assume the governorship, while Houstoun was listed as absent, presumably still trying to locate and arrest Zubly. The aftermath left only three delegates to vote on independence: Dr. Lyman Hall, Button Gwinnett, and George Walton. They unanimously voted in the affirmative for independence.

The ancestry of this patriot was of little distinction, and as such he is solely responsible for his rise to eminence. George Walton was born in 1740 in Frederick County, Virginia. As a youngster, he was orphaned, and because his family was desperately poor, he was left destitute. His education was extremely limited, and therefore, he was destined to be a common laborer. At age fourteen, George began an apprenticeship as a carpenter, but such pursuits did not satisfy his inquiring mind. His employer, who viewed academics to be a waste of time, kept young George's day filled with chores. However, during the evening, with the light of a candle, George read and studied, and his perseverance paid large dividends. Upon the completion of his apprenticeship, he moved to Georgia, where he commenced the study of law under the tutelage of Henry Young, a prominent barrister of that province.

At age thirty-four, during the height of political turbulence in the colonies, George Walton began his law practice. Henry Young, an ardent patriot, enlightened his pupil about the unconstitutional encroachments that Great Britain had perpetrated against the rights of the colonies. Through his tutor, Walton also became acquainted with fellow compatriots such as Lyman Hall and Button Gwinnett, whose great influence shaped his pliable mind to the ideology of republicanism and lit the fire of independence within his heart.

George Walton's bold opposition to the Tories earned him the confidence of the people of Georgia, and when they chose a strong Whig delegation for the Continental Congress, he was among them. Congress, at that time, had changed its venue to Baltimore because of the threat of attack from the British troops. Three days after Walton's arrival, Congress appointed him, along with Robert Morris and George Clymer, to the Secret Committee. That appointment was a tribute to his character, as it required the utmost integrity, since the committee was entrusted with almost unlimited discretion over the use of congressional finances. Walton proved to be a valuable member.

Walton left Congress in 1778 and returned to Georgia, where the state legislature had appointed him colonel of a regiment. He immediately joined with General Robert Howe in the defense of Savannah. During the siege, Colonel Walton was severely wounded by a musket shot to his thigh and taken captive. While being held with a wound that was thought to be fatal, he wrote the following to his wife: "Remember that you are the beloved wife of one who has made honour and reputation the ruling motive in every action of his life."[44] He did eventually recover and was subsequently released through a prisoner exchange.

In October 1779, Colonel Walton was appointed governor by the Georgia legislature, an office he held only briefly. In January the following year, he was reelected to Congress, where he remained for two additional years. Upon returning to his state, he was again elected governor, that time holding the office for a full term. Near the end of his term, the state legislature appointed him to the bench as chief justice, where he served faithfully until his death. He was also elected a US senator in 1798, but held the office for only one year before retiring from public life—except for his bench duties. George Walton died on February 2, 1804, in Augusta, Georgia, at the age of sixty-four.

Governor Walton elevated his lot in life from that of a carpenter's apprentice to the highest office in Georgia. By doing such, he leaves a shining example of what can be accomplished by determination and excellent character. He never accumulated many material belongings, but he and his wife lived in contentment at their small farm near Augusta. They had only one son, who was the source of great joy to his father. The remains of George Walton and Dr. Lyman Hall were later moved to a site of honor in Augusta. During the mid-nineteenth century, a lead monument was erected in their memory.

POSTSCRIPT

These life stories of the signers are typical of all those who risked everything for freedom. They were not crazed rebels possessed with ulterior motives. These elite family men were highly respected, well educated, and financially stable. They had everything, but valued liberty more. With unshakable reliance on divine Providence, they boldly declared the independence of the United States of America. When John Dickenson made his final argument against independence, he

> solemnly invoke[d] the Governor of the Universe, so to influence the minds of the members of Congress, that if the proposed measure was for the benefit of America, nothing he should say against it, might make the least impression.[45]

And it didn't. Congress believed that God had illuminated its collective mind. Having unity in thought, they acted in like manner and unanimously signed the Declaration of Independence. The Declaration was not born from ambitious politicians groping for wealth and power, but from the necessity to protect their inalienable, God-given right to self-government. Thus, after eleven years and three petitions, America had severed its political cord with its mother. Signing the Declaration was one thing, but the realization of independence would come at a much higher price. The sword would then have to determine whether they would be conquered provinces or free states.

The signers acted well within their rights—rights that were firmly founded in the laws of nature and God. However, such actions were tantamount to high treason in the courts of Great Britain. The signers were not naive optimists, for they understood that they were exposing themselves to the wrath of the most potent and vengeful military force in the world. They knew that if they failed in their quest for liberty, their lives, fortunes, and sacred honor would end up as nothing more than burned kindling on the ash heap of history.

Even in victory, their cost was great. Five signers were captured and thrown into British prisons, three died from hardships they suffered because of their support for independence or due to their military actions, one signer lost two of his sons on the battlefield, another had two of his sons captured and tortured, and at least a dozen had their homes pillaged or burned. When the young Confederacy could no longer financially support their military, they collectively made millions of dollars' worth of loans, even though most of them suspected that the loans would never be repaid—their suspicions proved correct. They stood tall and unwavering, as beacons for their oppressed countrymen. Throughout the long and perilous years of war, none of that noble band fell into moral degradation, nor were any diminished by their words or actions, none renounced the Declaration, and none complained about their sacrifice. They were men of integrity, and what they paid was no less than what they had pledged—their lives, their fortunes, and their sacred honor.

The Calm Before the Storm

George Washington

August 1776

After General Washington chased the British forces out of Boston Harbor, the Royal Navy sailed north to Halifax, where they took refuge while waiting for reinforcement from England. Near the end of June, General Howe—unwilling to wait any longer—sailed down the New England coast and, without opposition, took possession of Staten Island. In mid-July, a large portion of the Royal Navy finally arrived and joined them on the island. The combined British forces then equaled thirty-two thousand, outnumbering the Continental forces that were stationed on Long Island by more than ten thousand.

During the latter part of July, while Congress was cooped up in Carpenters' Hall—debating the topic of confederation and preparing for their signing ceremony—General Washington was fortifying his defenses on Long Island. Prior to any hostilities, the British attempted to negotiate a peaceful end to the standoff. They sent a white flag to Washington in order to begin some discussions. Their offer was nothing more that amnesty and a return to the way things had been. Washington replied, "Why should the people of a free country seek a pardon from another country?" The British returned to Staten Island, where they began planning their attack. The planning took many weeks—it was the calm before the storm.

As Washington was anticipating the impending attack, he addressed his army, reminding them that

> liberty, property, life, and honour, were all at stake; that upon their courage and conduct, rested the hopes of their bleeding and insulted country; that their wives, children, and parents, expected safety from them only; and that they had every reason to believe that Heaven would crown with success so just a cause.

He further added,

> The enemy will endeavor to intimidate by show and
> appearance, but remember they have been repulsed on
> various occasions by a few brave Americans—Their cause is
> bad; and their men are conscious of it . . . [46]

On August 28, 1776, the British attacked the Continental forces on
Long Island. Britain had launched a full-scale war on its insubordinate
American colonies.

SOURCE NOTES

Introduction

1. Christopher Columbus, *Christopher Columbus's Book of Prophecies*, trans. Kay Brigham (Barcelona, Spain: CLIE, 1990; Ft. Lauderdale: TSELF, 1991), 178-179, 182-183.
2. *Holy Trinity* at 466. See also Harvard's *Historical Collection*, vol. I, 119.
3. John Winthrop, "A Model of Christian Charity," in *The Winthrop Papers*, ed. Stewart Mitchell (Massachusetts Historical Society, 1931), vol. II, 292-295, 1630.
4. Hazard's *Historical Collection*, Vol. I, p. 463.
5. Hugh Talmage Lefler, ed. *North Carolina History* (Chapel Hill: University of North Carolina Press, 1934, 1956), 1.

Part I

1. Norman Cousins, *In God We Trust* (New York: Harper & Brothers, 1958), p. 24.
2. Harry Clinton Green and Mary Wolcott Green, *The Pioneer Mothers of America* (New York: G.P. Putnam's Sons, 1912), Vol. III, p. 178.
3. Cousins, *In God We Trust*, p. 38.
4. James Madison, *Notes of the Debates in the Federal Convention of 1787* (New York: Norton & Co., 1893), pp. 209-210.
5. Cousins, *In God We Trust*, p. 42.
6. David Barton, *The Bulletproof George Washington* (Aledo, Texas: Wallbuilders, 1998), pp. 45-47.
7. George Washington Parke Custis, *Recollections and Private Memoirs of Washington*, ed. Benson J. Lossing (New York: Derby & Jackson, 1860), pp. 303-304.
8. Green and Green, *The Pioneer Mothers of America*, Vol. II, p. 125.
9. Headley, *Washington and His Generals* (New York: Brader and Scribner, 1847), p. 109.
10. Green and Green, *The Pioneer Mothers of America*, Vol. II, p. 130.
11. Headley, *Washington and His Generals*, Vol. I, pp. 130-131.
12. William Wert Henry, *Patrick Henry: Life, Correspondence and Speeches* (Harrisonburg, VA: Sprinkle Publications, 1891), p. 83.

13. Moses Coit Tyler, *Patrick Henry* (Boston: Houghton Mifflin and Co., 1887), pp. 140-145.
14. A copy of his Last Will and Testament may be obtained from the state archives or the historical society.
15. M.E. Bradford, *The Trumpet Voice of Freedom: Patrick Henry of Virginia* (Marlborough, N.H.: The Plymouth Rock Foundation, 1991), p. i.
16. Tyler, *Patrick Henry,* p. 109, to Archibald Blair on January 8, 1799.
17. T.R. Fehrenbach, *Greatness to Spare* (Princeton, N.J.: D. Van Nostrand, 1968), p. 105.
18. A copy of his Last Will and Testament may be obtained from the state archives or the historical society.
19. John Dickinson, *The Political Writings of John Dickinson* (Wilmington, Del.: Bonsal and Niles, 1801), Vol. I, p. 111.
20. A copy of his Last Will and Testament may be obtained from the state archives and/or the historical society.
21. Mercy Otis Warren, *History of the Rise, Progress and Termination of the American Revolution* (Boston: Manning and Loring, 1805), Vol. I, pp. 50-51.
22. James Otis, *The Rights of the British Colonies Asserted and Proved* (London: J. Williams and J. Almon, 1766), pp. 11, 98.
23. John Witherspoon, *The Works of John Witherspoon* (Philadelphia: William W. Woodard, 1802), Vol. III, pp. 41-42.
24. B.J. Lossing, *Signers of the Declaration of Independence* (New York: Geo. F. Cooledge & Brother, 1848), p. 83.
25. Witherspoon, *The Works of John Witherspoon,* Vol. IV, p. 170.
26. Roger Schultz, *Covenanting in America: The Political Theology of John Witherspoon,* Master's Thesis (Deerfield, Ill.: Trinity Evangelical Divinity School, 1958), p. 149.
27. Witherspoon, *The Works of John Witherspoon,* 1815), Vol. V, pp. 276, 278.
28. Ibid., Vol. VII, p. 81.
29. Ibid., Vol. IV, p. 267.
30. Ibid., Vol. VII, p. 101.
31. Ibid., Vol. VIII, pp. 33, 38.
32. Ibid., Vol. IV, p. 265.

33. Benjamin Hart, *Faith and Freedom* (Christian Defense Fund, 1997), p. 262.
34. Ibid., p. 263.
35. Green and Green, *The Pioneer Mothers of America*, Vol. III, p. 68.
36. Ibid., p. 69.
37. Lossing, *Signers of the Declaration of Independence,* p. 35.
38. Samuel Adams, *The Life and Public Service of Samuel Adams,* ed. William V. Wells (Boston: Little, Brown, and Company, 1865), Vol. I, p. 504.
39. Charles E. Kistler, *This Nation Under God* (Boston: The Gorham Press, 1942), p. 71.
40. A copy of his Last Will and Testament may be obtained from the state archives or the historical society.
41. Samuel Adams, *The Writings of Samuel Adams,* ed. Harry Alonzo Cushing (New York: G.P. Putnam's Sons, 1904), Vol. IV, p. 38.
42. Ibid., p. 86.

Part II

1. John Adams, Abigail Adams, *Letters of John Adams, Addressed to His Wife,* ed. Charles Francis Adams (Boston: Charles C. Little and James Brown, 1841), Vol. I, pp. 23-24.
2. Thomas Y. Rhodes, *The Battlefields of the Revolution* (Philadelphia: J.W. Bradley, 1860), pp. 36-39.
3. David Ramsay, *The History of the American Revolution* (Philadelphia: R. Aitken, 1789), Vol. I, p. 131.
4. Ibid., p. 130.
5. Fehrenbach, *Greatness to Spare,* p. 213.
6. *Journals of . . . Massachusetts* (Concord, April 15, 1775), pp. 144-145.
7. Ethan Allen, *A Narrative of Colonial Ethan Allen's Captivity* (Burlington, Vermont: H. Johnson and Co., 1838), pp. 17-18.
8. Ramsay, *The History of the American Revolution,* Vol. I, p. 190.
9. Ibid., p. 203.
10. David Ramsay, *The Life of George Washington* (Baltimore: Joseph Cushing, 1807), pp. 30-31.
11. Moncure D. Conway, *George Washington's Rules of Civility* (BN Publishing, 2009), pp. 178-180.

12. John N. Norton, *Life of George Washington* (1870), p. 34.
13. Headley, *Washington and His Generals*, Vol. I, p. 134.
14. Ibid., p. 140.
15. Ibid., p. 144.
16. Ramsay, *The Life of George Washington*, p. 31.
17. *The World Book Encyclopedia*, 18 Vols. (Chicago: Field Enterprises, 1957), Vol. XI, p. 5324.
18. Cousins, *In God We Trust*, p. 391.
19. George Washington, *The Writings of George Washington, 39 Volumes*, ed. John C. Fitzpatrick (Washington DC: United States Government Printing Office, 1931-44), 4:297.
20. Cousins, *In God We Trust*, p. 390.
21. Benson J. Lossing, *Eminent Americans* (New York: American Book Exchange, 1881), p. 229.
22. Warren, *History of the Rise*, Vol. I, p. 138.
23. Benjamin Hart, *Faith and Freedom* (Christian Defense Fund, 1997), p. 280.
24. Ibid., p. 281.
25. Headley, *Washington and His Generals*, Vol. II, p. 103.
26. Ramsay, *The History of the American Revolution*, Vol. I, p. 247.
27. Washington, *The Writings of George Washington*, 4:489.
28. Lossing, *Signers of the Declaration of Independence*, p. 12.
29. Ibid., p. 168.
30. Ibid., p. 171.
31. *Journals of . . . Congress* (1907), Vol. IX, 1777, pp. 854-855.
32. Fehrenbach, *Greatness to Spare*, p. 209.
33. Lossing, *Signers of the Declaration of Independence*, p. 173.
34. Fehrenbach, *Greatness to Spare*, p. 183.
35. Ibid., p. 184.
36. Ibid., p. 185.
37. Ibid., p. 185.
38. Headley, *Washington and His Generals*, Vol. II, p. 91.
39. Ibid., pp. 97-98.
40. Lossing, *Eminent Americans*, p. 263.
41. Washington, *The Writings of George Washington*, 5:211.
42. Ibid., 5:245.
43. Lossing, *Signers of the Declaration of Independence*, p. 254.

44. Herbert Lockyer, *Last Words of Saints and Sinners* (Grand Rapids, Mich.: Kregel, 1969), p.98.
45. Lossing, *Signers of the Declaration of Independence*, p. 182.
46. Ibid., p. 183.
47. Thomas Jefferson, *Notes on the State of Virginia* (Philadelphia: Mathew Carey, 1794), p. 237, Query XVIII.
48. Thomas Jefferson, *The Writings of Thomas Jefferson*, ed. Albert Ellery Bergh (Washington DC: The Thomas Jefferson Memorial Association, 1904), Vol. XIV, p. 385.

Part III

1. Lossing, *Signers of the Declaration of Independence*, p. 21.
2. Benjamin Pierce, *A History of Harvard University* (Cambridge, MA: Brown, Shattuck, and Co., 1833), Appendix, p. 5.
3. A copy of his Last Will and Testament may be obtained from the state archives or the historical society.
4. Stephan Hopkins, *The Rights of Colonies Examined* (Providence, RI: William Goddard, 1765), pp. 23-34.
5. Charles A. Goodrich, *Lives of the Signers* (New York: William Reed & Co., 1829), p. 153.
6. John Sanderson, *Biography of the Signers of the Declaration of Independence* (Philadelphia: R.W. Pomeroy, 1824), Vol. VI, pp. 253, 260.
7. Lossing, *Eminent Americans*, p. 320.
8. Green and Green, *The Pioneer Mothers of America*, Vol. III, pp. 102-103.
9. Fehrenbach, *Greatness to Spare*, p. 50.
10. Green and Green, *The Pioneer Mothers of America*, Vol. III, pp. 141-142.
11. Lossing, *Signers of the Declaration of Independence*, pp. 86-87.
12. William Livingston, *The Pioneer Papers of William Livingston* (Trenton: New Jersey Historical Commission, 1979), Vol. I, p. 161.
13. A copy of his Last Will and Testament may be obtained from the state archives or the historical society.
14. Fehrenbach, *Greatness to Spare*, p. 65.
15. A copy of his Last Will and Testament may be obtained from the state archives or the historical society.
16. Lossing, *Signers of the Declaration of Independence*, p. 102.

17. Ibid., p.103.
18. Fehrenbach, *Greatness to Spare*, p. 116.
19. Green and Green, *The Pioneer Mothers of America*, Vol. III, p. 202.
20. Lossing, *Signers of the Declaration of Independence*, p. 122.
21. Ibid., p. 156.
22. Ibid., p. 156.
23. Fehrenbach, *Greatness to Spare*, p. 134.
24. Ibid., p. 20.
25. Green and Green, *The Pioneer Mothers of America*, Vol. III, p. 225.
26. Lossing, *Signers of the Declaration of Independence*, p. 161.
27. From an autographed letter written from Charles Carroll to Charles W. Wharton, Esq. (Aledo, Texas: Wallbuilders, 1825).
28. Bernard C. Steiner, *The Life and Correspondence of James McHenry* (Cleveland: The Burrows Brothers Co., 1907), p. 475.
29. Lossing, *Signers of the Declaration of Independence*, p. 200.
30. Fehrenbach, *Greatness to Spare*, p. 228
31. Ibid., p. 203.
32. Ibid., p. 207.
33. David Barton, *The Signing of the Declaration of Independence* (poster), (Aledo, Texas: Wallbuilders, 1998).
34. Fehrenbach, *Greatness to Spare*, p. 212.
35. Ibid., p. 214.
36. Davis Newton Lott, *The Inaugural Address of the American Presidents* (New York: Holt, Rinehart and Winston, 1961), p. 86.
37. Edmund Fuller and David E. Green, *God in the White House—The Faiths of American Presidents* (New York: Crown Publishers, Inc., 1968), p. 155.
38. Fehrenbach, *Greatness to Spare*, p. 184.
39. Green and Green, *The Pioneer Mothers of America*, Vol. III, pp. 271-272.
40. Fehrenbach, *Greatness to Spare*, p. 171.
41. Ibid., pp. 167-168.
42. Lossing, *Signers of the Declaration of Independence*, p. 222.
43. Green and Green, *The Pioneer Mothers of America*, Vol. III, p. 227.
44. Ibid., pp. 278-279.
45. Ramsay, *The History of the American Revolution*, Vol. I, p. 318.
46. Ramsay, *The Life of George Washington*, pp. 39-40.

BIBLIOGRAPHY
Primary Sources of Research

The Life of George Washington, Commander and Chief of the Armies of the United States of America, Throughout the War which Established Their Independence; and First President of the United States
1807 — David Ramsay, MD

This book traces the life of George Washington—from his childhood to his death, and every major event in between: the French and Indian War, Virginia politics, his agricultural pursuits, his involvement in our nation's struggle for freedom, the Revolutionary War, his involvement in the establishment of our Constitution, his presidency, and his retirement.

The Life of George Washington
Special Edition for Schools
1849 — John Marshall

Within eight years of the death of George Washington in 1799, John Marshall, who later became the chief justice of the US Supreme Court, published his authoritative five-volume biography. In 1833, Marshall reduced his work into a 400-page, single-volume "special edition" to be used as a textbook for schools and colleges.

Washington and His Generals
in Two Volumes
1847 — J.T. Headley

This work describes the predominant characters and events surrounding the armed conflict of the American Revolution. In-depth biographical studies of General Washington's subordinate generals are included.

Eminent Americans
1881 — Benson J. Lossing

The lives of over four hundred eminent Americans are chronicled in this biographical encyclopedia. Its brief sketches begin with America's earliest settlers and end at the date of printing.

The History of the American Revolution
in Two Volumes
1789 — David Ramsay, MD

This book appeared in 1789 during an enthusiastic celebration of nationhood. It is the first American national history written by an American revolutionary and printed in America. Ramsay was an active participant in many of the events of the period. He was a soldier, physician, and a member of the Continental Congress. Ramsay discusses the events that founded America, from the outbreak of the turbulence in the 1760s to the inset of Washington's administration.

History of the Rise, Progress and Termination of the American Revolution
in Two Volumes
1805 — Mercy Otis Warren

Mercy Otis Warren, the sister of James Otis and wife of James Warren (president of the Massachusetts Provincial Congress), was perhaps the most formidable female intellectual in eighteenth-century America. This work is a comprehensive study of the events of the American Revolution and the establishment of the post-Confederation government.

Biographical Sketches of the Lives of the Signers
of the Declaration of American Independence
1848 — Benson J. Lossing

This compilation provides a glimpse into the lives of the fifty-six men who signed the Declaration—that illustrious band of freedom fighters who pledged their lives, fortunes, and sacred honor for our liberty.

The Pioneer Mothers of America
in Three Volumes
1912 — Harry Clinton Green and Mary Wolcott Green, A.B.

This collection of biographies helps to paint a more complete picture of the Founding Fathers, giving us insight into their family values and domestic pursuits.

INDEX

ABOUT THE AUTHOR

In 1986, Leslie Mironuck immigrated to the United States from Canada and has taken full advantage of the Land of Opportunity. He became a real estate broker and now owns multiple real estate offices. He also owns a restaurant, a Bed & Breakfast, a property management company, and large portfolio of rental properties.

Mr. Mironuck's life journey has given him a unique perspective on America. For the first 28 years of his life, he lived outside the country, viewing America from afar. However, during that time he often vacationed in the United States while visiting his relatives—his maternal ancestors have lived in Missouri since the mid 1800s. During those visits, he caught a glimpse of American culture. Then in 1986, he and his young family immigrated to the United States and made St. Louis their home. While raising his family in the heartland, he had the opportunity to gain an internal view of America. Mr. Mironuck has since reconciled his various perspectives of America—as a foreigner, as a frequent visitor, and finally as a permanent resident. Part of that reconciliation process included his quest to learn the secret of America's success . . . to answer his question: what makes the United States such a great nation? Part of his quest led him through a self-study of America's history.

During his study of America's colonial era, Mr. Mironuck discovered that the "history" being taught in our public schools differed greatly from the actual historic events. Equally alarming, he discovered that most of the main participants—the Founding Fathers—were simply absent from that curriculum. It appeared to him that the revisionists had been hard at work, putting forth their new, politically correct version of history. In this three-volume series, Mr. Mironuck offers an accurate record of America's founding era.

Special Note from the Author

Understanding and embracing the values of America's Founding Fathers is where true patriotism begins. It is my desire to help preserve the honorable reputation of America's early patriots and to promote their values, beliefs, and characteristics. If America will adopt the Founding Father's attributes, I believe a more elevated society will result.

This is the first of three books in *The American Patriots Series*. The next two are:

Liberty or Death
Profiles of the Founding Fathers
1776 - 1786

Dawn of a Nation
Profiles of the Founding Fathers
1787 - 1799

Please visit my publisher's website, www.LafayettePublishers.com for the latest historical updates, news about these two new titles, and events and activities across the country.

You can sign up to receive updates, special promotions, and announcements about events . . . and be among the first to receive the next book in *The American Patriot Series*. You may also order an autographed copy of this book.

Want to know even more about our Founding Fathers? Check out my blog and social media sites found on the website.

Have a comment or want to respond?
Contact me directly at Les@LafayettePublishers.com

Les Mironuck